"Clark puts into words and theory what every experienced youth ministry leader knows intuitively! *Adoptive Church* lays out both a vision and a strategy for fully integrating young people into faith communities. It describes a larger context for youth ministry and provides a new guide for pastoral ministry not only with young people but also with the entire faith community."

—**Bob McCarty**, pastoral trainer and consultant in Catholic youth ministry; Catholic University of America and University of Dallas

"The phrase 'a must-read for church leaders' is often used to promote a book. Honestly, when I read such words, they come across as presumptuous and leave me questioning the authority of the author. Well, *Adoptive Church* is a *must-read* for church leaders desiring to engage today's adolescent community in ministry. It is essential reading for both youth workers and senior church leaders. Clark has been a mentor and friend of mine for many years. His authority to speak into the life of the church comes from a lifetime of study, engagement, and ministry in the trenches. *Adoptive Church* will challenge, guide, and empower churches serious about ministering to today's adolescent culture."

—**David Wayne Fraze**, Lubbock Christian University

"It is fitting that Clark publishes *Adoptive Church* as he transitions into a ministerial role that will permit him to practice the tenets of this book. For many decades Clark has empowered the church to live out its God-given vocation to love young people. His efforts have challenged and empowered generations of youth ministry educators and practitioners. *Adoptive Church* does not disappoint. Insightful, confessional, and pastoral, Clark's latest work—rooted in years of practical experience, research, and thoughtful analysis—will bless churches for years to come."

—**Steven Bonner**, Lipscomb University

"This beautifully challenging book results from Clark's long experience of reflecting upon, analyzing, and serving the church. In *Adoptive Church*, Clark offers a metaphor, theology, vision, and trajectory—a practical, intentional way that leads to being a nurturing and empowering household of God. This is deep ecclesiology. It is a way of being church, a church for which many step back and examine our theology and to refocus on being church—for youth, f

—**Fr. Reynold Furrell,**

Youth, Family, and Culture Series

Chap Clark, series editor

The Youth, Family, and Culture series examines the broad categories involved in studying and caring for the needs of the young and is dedicated to the preparation and vocational strengthening of those who are committed to the spiritual development of adolescents.

ADOPTIVE CHURCH

CREATING AN ENVIRONMENT
WHERE **EMERGING GENERATIONS** BELONG

CHAP CLARK

Foreword by STEVEN ARGUE

Baker Academic

a division of Baker Publishing Group
Grand Rapids, Michigan

© 2018 by Chap Clark

Published by Baker Academic
a division of Baker Publishing Group
PO Box 6287, Grand Rapids, MI 49516-6287
www.bakeracademic.com

Printed in the United States of America

Library of Congress Cataloging-in-Publication Data
Names: Clark, Chap, 1954– author.
Title: Adoptive church : creating an environment where emerging generations belong / Chap Clark.
Description: Grand Rapids, MI : Baker Academic, a division of Baker Publishing Group, [2018] | Series: Youth, family, and culture series
Identifiers: LCCN 2018020595 | ISBN 9780801098925 (paper)
Subjects: LCSH: Church work with youth. | Adoption (Theology)
Classification: LCC BV4447 .C5115 2018 | DDC 259/.23—dc23
LC record available at https://lccn.loc.gov/2018020595

In keeping with biblical principles of creation stewardship, Baker Publishing Group advocates the responsible use of our natural resources. As a member of the Green Press Initiative, our company uses recycled paper when possible. The text paper of this book is composed in part of post-consumer waste.

18   19   20   21   22   23   24   7   6   5   4   3   2   1

This book is for Dee: my partner, my friend, and my joy. Through the years we have loved, learned, and served together. Now we get the chance to influence and journey alongside a community that is trying to figure out what it means to be authentically faithful to God's call and therefore to learn to live as an adoptive family. The greatest joy? We get to do this together!

CONTENTS

FOREWORD

Where do all the great ministry leaders go when they grow older? They're still here—loving, serving, leading, and advocating for young people regardless of what position they hold. They're still convinced that the gospel remains great news for every generation. They're pro-church even though they've seen and experienced both its beauty and ugliness. They're a unique breed. They're people like Chap Clark.

As a young youth pastor, I had the benefit of learning from Chap through his writing and speaking. His ideas gave me helpful language and vision for the ministry experiences I encountered. As I matured and our paths crossed at conferences, two things struck me about Chap: he loves young people, and he loves people who love young people.

More recently, I have had the distinct opportunity to be Chap's colleague at Fuller Theological Seminary. While his work on campus and around the country is known by many, I personally witnessed the value he placed on harmonizing academic rigor with a pastoral heart. His influence on countless master's and doctoral students is profound, and I believe we will feel the ripple effect of Chap's investment well into the next generation of leaders.

Adoptive Church is not his next, new idea. In fact, Chap would say the concept is quite old, but it has yet to be realized in congregational contexts. While youth ministry has become an essential element for most churches, it has typically morphed into a closed system that gets isolated from the congregation and outsourced to a youth pastor or a few caring adults. Such a system leaves senior leaders and youth leaders working in tandem but not together. Research indicates that an intergenerational dynamic is essential for influencing the way congregations form young people. Chap seeks to operationalize an intergenerational vision through an adoptive lens that reorients the roles of pastor, youth pastor, mentor, and young person as part of the family of God. His ideas will offer readers the helpful first steps they are looking for while calling them to make additional moves that may challenge their deeply held assumptions.

As you read this book also pay attention to its tone. What I have always appreciated about Chap is his unique ability to remind youth ministry rookies and veterans why they do what they do. His insights are encased with inspiration that perpetually says, "You love young people? So do I. Let's do this!" Hear Chap's voice as one who is more interested in cheering you on than dragging you down. I believe his encouragement has kept many youth ministry leaders from throwing in the towel.

Many pastors find their way into academics (I'm one of them). A select few find their way from the academy to the church. What I find especially unique about this book is that it is written by a tenured professor who has felt drawn to the pastorate to flesh out his adoptive ideas within his own local congregation. As you read Chap's words, recognize that he is sweating out these convictions with you, cheering you on, and speaking a phrase that saved my own ministry soul numerous times, "I love you. You're the best."

Steven Argue

ACKNOWLEDGMENTS

This book is the outcome of a lifetime of serving the young in the name of Christ. There are so many who have factored in to this project, for I have gleaned from hundreds—if not thousands—of people and sources that have influenced my thinking. So I acknowledge first that large pool of dedicated men and women that have served our Lord by loving the young and their families. You have shaped me far more than I could ever know.

There are also those specific people and places along the way that deserve an additional shout-out.

Young Life and the Young Life staff: I have been reared in the ministry and ethos of this global organization that remains focused on one thing—to introduce every young person to Jesus Christ. The Young Life family helped me to know the biblical Jesus, weaned me into the church, and invited me to join in their mission. Although I stopped receiving a paycheck many years ago, I have never stopped being one of you in this incredible mission to the young. Thank you for teaching me that every kid matters and is worth our very best thinking and effort.

The parish youth ministry family: Early on, my high school Young Life leader was clear: "You've gotten close to Christ with us, now give yourself to becoming part of his family." This early experience convinced me that no matter what we do in the name of youth or emerging adult ministry, our goal must be helping the young to see their place and their home within the body of Christ. For every youth worker who has ever served the young in the church, thanks for your dedication and the hard-won lessons that God has used to shape me.

To my friends and colleagues in Christian leadership: I have been so profoundly humbled to have been included in your guild. From being invited to serve and train on behalf of Youth Specialties, to inclusion on the stellar faculties of Denver and Fuller seminaries, to the chance to wrestle alongside insightful and dedicated colleagues who have led the way in youth and emerging adult ministry, I am deeply moved that you let me in the door with you. And to all who have invited me to write and speak all these years, I am indebted to you for letting me work out my understanding of this vital calling alongside you.

And to those who have specifically helped with the adoptive ministry movement: I am so grateful for the partnership of Steve Rabey, Mindy Coates Smith, Tom Combes; all the DMin students over the last few years; and PhD grads Jinna Jin and David Doong.

Welcome to the Adoptive Church

In Christ, we are each an essential part of an intentionally adoptive community that passes its heritage through the generations. . . . We are indwelt by the Holy Spirit and function as the incarnation of Jesus Christ to one another.

—Scott Wilcher, *The Orphaned Generation*[1]

I f you could give me one word that would help me figure out how to do youth ministry well, what would that be?" asked the twenty-three-year-old youth ministry major who had just graduated and was about to start her new job.

A self-described "youth group kid," she had grown up in church groups, had read many key books, had heard speakers at ministry conventions, and had been trained at one of the best Christian schools. Now she really wanted to know how to make ministry matter.

"Adoptive ministry," I said.

"Um, so, do we *adopt* kids?"

"No, God adopts them when they come to faith. And the key is he adopts everyone who comes to him. We just get the privilege of helping young people live into the gift that God has for them. That's youth ministry. That's the church—the *adoptive church*!"

Maybe you're new to youth ministry and, like this enthusiastic, young youth worker, have come to this book wanting to get at the essence of the important calling you have answered.

Or perhaps you are a seasoned veteran of youth ministry who's looking for an overarching concept that could pull together all your years of study, work, and engagement with kids.

Or maybe you're somewhere in the middle: a parent, a pastor, or someone else who has witnessed plenty of youth ministry hits and misses. You're committed to ministry but realize things could be better, so you're open to a new conversation.

Whatever your reason for joining in the discussion, I want to welcome you and thank you for taking a step into this adventure I call adoptive youth ministry. It's not so much a new way of *doing* youth ministry as a new way of *thinking* about and then *framing* the work of youth ministry.

For years I taught and wrote that the point of youth ministry was not only to help young people come to know and ultimately trust and follow Jesus Christ but also to then help them connect to the larger body of Christ. I referred to this as "assimilating" the young into the body of Christ.[2]

A few years ago in an intensive doctor of ministry class at Fuller Seminary, one of the students challenged the word *assimilate*. The discussion became focused on the question, Whose church is it, anyway? And why should young people have to "assimilate" in order to be welcomed and received?

That started me on a mission to search the Scriptures and discover what the Bible says about who we are together. Two passages shouted out for my attention: "To all who did receive him, to those who believed in his name, he gave the right to become children of God" and "The Spirit you received brought about your adoption to sonship. And by him we cry, '*Abba*, Father'" (John 1:12; Rom. 8:15).

In other words, once upon a time you and I were lost and orphaned, but in Christ, God made a way for us to come home as his adopted children. Adoptive youth ministry is simply helping kids live into that truth.

Throughout this journey, several things have fundamentally changed how I think about youth ministry. First, children, adolescents, and emerging adults are not the "church of tomorrow" but are members in the church of today. Other leaders have discussed this issue, but adoptive ministry addresses it head-on.

Second, our main job is to help kids to be received, nurtured, and appropriately empowered to live into their place at the feasting table of the King (Matt. 22).

Third, youth ministry must be a *bridge* that reaches out and touches isolated, disconnected, and fragmented kids, encouraging them to accept Christ's love and the love of God's people.

These three aha moments form the basis of this book and the earlier multiauthored textbook *Adoptive Youth Ministry* (Baker Academic, 2016). In this book, we will flesh out what this means in shaping a youth ministry program that leads into lifelong faith among siblings in the body of Christ. We will begin with the goal of adoptive youth ministry, then look at how to structure ministry in your context that will lead to the goal, and finish with the fundamental practices that will keep your ministry vibrant not only for the young people in your community but also for the congregation as a whole.

As you read, you might find yourself asking questions about some of the wording or concepts that are sprinkled throughout the book. Some of these are common words used differently (such as *adoption*). Others might represent brand-new ways of thinking about our life together as followers of Christ or even as leaders. I have provided a quick guide in the appendix titled "Adoptive Church 101" that you might want to dog-ear, or even read before you begin, so you are able to track with the essential components of adoptive youth ministry.

One last thing before you join in the conversation. My career has been primarily focused on training people who care for the young—parents, youth workers, educators, therapists—and helping them understand and serve the young well. The lens through which I have seen our work in relation to the needs of kids has been youth ministry. My advocacy for the young has never changed, but throughout the process of considering who we are together as God's household, I have come to see that by looking only through the lens of one particular group, I have missed out on seeing the whole. Adoptive youth ministry sees the church, and who we are together as God's household, and then creates a pathway for the young to enter into that family through youth ministry.

Adoptive ministry sees the church as Christ's body, the household of God, the home for everyone whom God has called. Our task is to develop the kind of strategy and create the kind of environment where young people can not only envision themselves as vital members of that flawed-yet-redeemed family but also be put on a pathway to actually experiencing this reality. That is adoptive youth ministry.

So buckle up and prepare to encounter some new ways of thinking, but also be ready to be encouraged by the journey ahead with students and young adults. Youth ministry as a movement has been on this trajectory for years. The adoptive church is youth ministry with a destination: the household of God.

1

Creating an Adoptive Youth Ministry

It is not enough to connect [teenagers] to a task, but to empower the church to help students to live into their mutual adoption as members of the family of God. As I reflect on this, I continue to dream of ways to make this more of a reality at our church.

—Parent newsletter from a youth pastor, April 2, 2017

Youth pastors were gathered for a morning seminar when I gave them the following scenario. You are applying for a job at a midsized church where you would follow a series of part-time youth directors who weren't ever able to get much going. Now the church wants to start over from scratch with a new youth leader. During your interview, one of the church's leaders says to you, "Blank slate here. If you were to come to our church, what questions would you ask yourself, and why?"

"OK," I told the youth workers, "you've got five minutes to write down your answers."

They furrowed their brows, wrote their questions, shared in small groups, and then voiced their opinions in a large group discussion. The discussion was lively, animated, and occasionally contentious, and everyone seemed deeply engaged. For the first few minutes, the youth workers focused their questions on the church's students:

- How do we get them to come (to events, church, camps, etc.)?
- How do we get kids to care (about the program, God, each other, us)?
- How do we get students to want to grow in their faith?
- How do we get nonchurched students in the door?

Soon, however, the group shifted to talking almost entirely about the church, asking questions like these:

- How involved are adults in the lives of kids? How involved do adults *want* to be in the lives of students?
- How do the older folks feel about the students in the church?
- Do students like going to church services? Do they feel welcomed and appreciated?
- Do adults—staff and laity—believe that teenagers have something to offer the church?

As I moderated the discussion, I was struck by how questions about these two areas—the students and the church—gradually converged into one. Most seemed to agree that to get students to care about the youth ministry, or about the church, or even about Jesus Christ, adults had to care about the students.

One of the elder leaders (he was all of forty years old!) stood up and said, "So, for us to lead kids to Christ, we also have to find a way to lead them into a church community that wants and values them."

Heads nodded. We went to prayer. I thanked God for the discussion.

Youth ministry at its best is a reflection of the church—what I call the adoptive church—reaching out to a generation of young people who wonder where they fit. Our fundamental desire is to help each of our students come into a vibrant, genuine relationship with Jesus that will last a lifetime.

For that to happen, they need to somehow locate themselves within a community that not only reflects their faith but also enhances and deepens it. To be committed to loving kids in Christ's name means somehow helping them to find their home among God's people, the local church.

This is our biblical and theological calling. I call this adoptive youth ministry. And discussions like the one I had with those youth workers show why more leaders are embracing the adoptive ministry model.

Adoptive Youth Ministry: Bringing Together the Church and Kids

The concept of adoption isn't new or radical. We've all known people who have adopted a child, or have been adopted themselves, or both. It's easy for us to envision youth ministry as "adoption" because of what goes into the process of adoption: a child who, for whatever reason, didn't have a family finds a new, welcoming family that wants and loves this child.

I've found that people can quickly and easily embrace adoptive ministry concepts, such as having students "adopt" elderly adults in the church, or having church families "adopt" young people who lack supportive families.

"Adoptive" offers a good way to think about, describe, and strategize youth ministry. As John tells us, "To all who did receive him, to those who believed in his name, he gave the right to become children of God" (John 1:12). Paul picks up this lingo five times in his letters, reminding us that we who follow Christ have been "adopted to sonship" (or daughtership)[1] and are now able to call God not only our

Father but "Abba," a term used by Paul twice that "conveyed both a sense of warm intimacy and also filial respect."[2]

In the adoptive church we don't actually "adopt" each other; rather, we recognize that each of us, in Christ, has been adopted by God. This changes everything about what it means for us to be together as a body. We are, as followers of Jesus, officially related to each other. We are spiritual siblings. Christian kin.

The lively discussion I had with those youth workers that morning focused on relationships, particularly relationships between adults and students. Adoptive youth ministry is an intentional and strategic process for creating the kind of environment where young people can feel valued and included and where adults can receive and empower the young. It is based on the theological truth that whoever is "in Christ"[3] is an adopted sibling of everyone else "in Christ," regardless of gender, ethnicity, location in the world, denomination, or even, yes, age. Old Christians are big brothers and sisters of young Christians.

This is the foundation on which adoptive youth ministry thrives. The goal of adoptive ministry is that everything we think, do, and plan should enhance those familial relationships. Let's see how that can play out in real life.

Essentials of Adoptive Youth Ministry

In the first book that talked about adoptive ministry, *Youth Ministry in the 21st Century: Five Views*, as editor and contributor I made the case for adoptive youth ministry. A few months later I contributed to and edited the first full book on this idea, *Adoptive Youth Ministry: Integrating Emerging Generations into the Family of Faith*. There I laid out the basic premise of what it means to see the ultimate end of youth ministry being young people deeply integrated in God's household on earth known as the local church. In the first two chapters of that book I explain the concept of adoptive ministry, and then twenty-three other authors—all respected and experienced youth ministry leaders—write about how they envision this happening in a given aspect of youth ministry. Although the contributors had various levels of familiarity with the specifics of adoptive ministry, the book's value is that everyone had the same outcome in mind.

This book, in contrast to the first two, is designed to help you explore how adoptive youth ministry can strengthen and enhance your current ministry to both young people and the broader church body. First, I set the stage by explaining the rationale and goal behind adoptive youth ministry as a framework for doing youth ministry. Next, I will help you take steps to implement the kind of contextual ministry strategy that you and your community need in order to connect young people with the local body. Then, I will help you integrate best practices that enhance adoptive ministry for the long haul. Finally, we will explore ways to bring about change in faith communities that may be resistant to change.

These approaches can help you create the kind of environments where young people's faith and life can flourish as they become more integrated, loved, and empowered as members of God's household on earth.

First, let's examine the four essentials of an adoptive youth ministry and an adoptive church.

Living according to Our Mutual Adoption in Christ

In John 6, when Jesus was asked what "work" God required of people, he simply said, "The work of God is this: to believe in the one he has sent" (John 6:29). As mentioned, in John 1:12 we read that whoever has believed in Jesus is given "the right [i.e., privilege, reality] to become children of God" by God's adoption. This means, of course, that every person who sincerely desires to belong to Christ has been adopted by God and is therefore a member of God's household (Eph. 2:19).

Adoptive ministry nicely summarizes what it means to be adopted into the family of God as children of God. Once we're adopted, we

live according to our adoption by learning how all of us can live together. Since it takes a lifetime to shed the residue of the past and embrace what God has declared is true about us, we need not only each
other but also the Holy Spirit in our midst to prompt and empower
our calling.

The Strong Must Seek Out and Help the Weak

What do most siblings do when one of their brothers or sisters
is struggling or hurting? They gather around and help the afflicted
sibling. That kind of care should be the model in God's family.

It is not up to the weak, vulnerable, or disempowered to initiate a
connection with the powerful and dominant. Those who feel excluded
to the fringes of a congregation or Christian community assume they
don't have the social capital to approach those who are reigning in
the center. We can't expect the vulnerable to engage the strong, so
it's up to the more mature and interconnected family members to
engage those who are weak or disempowered.

Jesus modeled this approach in John 13 when he washed the disciples' feet, even those of his betrayer, Judas! The strong must help
the weak, particularly in adoptive youth ministry. Adolescents and
emerging adults who are in transition can feel weak and vulnerable
when confronted with a family they're not a part of. Those who are
older, more established, and more secure in church congregations
must build bridges of trust and inclusion with those who are young,
less established, or less secure.

Ministry to the Vulnerable Is a Bridge

In the introduction I described adoptive youth ministry as a *bridge*
ministry. A bridge ministry is one that exists not for its own sake or
the pleasure of its own constituents but rather for the sake of those
served. People involved in bridge ministries see themselves as the
connecting point between young people seeking a place in the world
and members of the family of God.

In a sense, any ministry can be a bridge ministry. Ministry to singles is a bridge to people who don't feel like they fit into a family-values environment. Ministry to the elderly provides a bridge to people who often feel cut off from the world and other people. Divorce recovery ministry is a bridge to people who've suffered tremendous sorrow and pain in their most intimate relationships.

At any time, there are needy populations observing our congregation to see if there's a place for them. Targeted ministry to specific, neglected (or underreached) populations is helpful and necessary, especially if trust with those who are in that population needs to be developed. Because a bridge ministry takes people from one world into another, a solid strategy and targeted programming are invaluable.

The Role of Leaders Is to Include and Empower Everyone

When all members of a community begin to see themselves as siblings, there may be a sense that some leadership roles will fade away. But let's not confuse roles with status. A leader may have an important role in a community that may entail using authority and power in the fulfillment of their calling. But this doesn't mean the leader is more valuable, worthy, gifted, or talented than any other member.

We have roles because in our fallen world we need people to use their particular gifts and resources to provide structure so our family can function harmoniously. Hierarchy and the appropriate use of organizational power are necessary in any group or system. Yet in a group of siblings, no leader matters more than the lowliest, newest member. Adoptive ministry needs strong, humble leaders with accountability in place to prevent the leaders from becoming self-important to the point where they fail to recognize who is being left behind. These leaders must make sure that the vulnerable are nurtured, empowered, and included in the church body.

What Adoptive Ministry Is and Is Not

Having outlined the four essentials, let me clarify three things that adoptive youth ministry is and is not.

Adoptive Ministry Is a Family, Not an Adoption Agency

Don't get me wrong, folks. I am employing an analogy, not declaring that your youth ministry must transform itself into a legal adoption agency.

Adoptive ministry doesn't mean I adopt another person into my biological family. Rather, it means that followers of Jesus determine to live out our adoption in God's family together as a community. I'm describing a way of thinking and living. Because we have all been adopted by a loving God as his children, we need to grow into and help each other discover what that means.

Adoptive Ministry Is a Unified Family, Not a Collection of Disconnected Subgroups

Many ministry leaders love the fact that churches often function as a set of separate entities (men's ministry, women's ministry, worship, children, youth, college, singles, seniors, etc.). But adoptive ministry leaders revel in working with the whole family of God.

The separation and disconnection caused by putting people into distinct groups have taken a severe toll on the unity Christ said should characterize his body ("This is my command: Love each other," John 15:17). Often what is talked about in youth group is different from, or even at odds with, what the elderly talk about in their group. All too often ministries exist for their own sake, and this is the opposite of adoptive ministry.

This is especially true when it comes to adolescents and emerging adults. Our calling is to connect each and every one to the whole congregation in real and meaningful ways. So while inviting high school students to join a men's retreat may be a good strategy so that the young men begin to connect with older men in the congregation, you also need a bridge strategy to connect these young men to the larger church family, where they build more relationships with more members of the body.

Adoptive Ministry Is Building Family Connections, Not Piling on Programs

The heart of adoptive ministry is to reach out to anyone who is vulnerable, on the outside of the group, or who worries that they will never be accepted as an equal member. Solid programs and structures can help this bridge process as long as we don't allow ourselves to confuse programs with connections. Most young people by definition feel vulnerable and worry about acceptance, at least at times, even in the church. This vulnerability is what needs to be addressed, and this is the point of adoptive youth ministry.

It often takes a while for outsiders to join a community and feel comfortable there. Your existing programming and structures offer newcomers a framework through which they can naturally enter into the broader life of the group. Leaders need to offer focused programming while simultaneously moving every member toward greater inclusion in the larger body.

Foundations of Adoptive Church Ministry: Three Core Competencies

Adoptive Church is designed as a nuts-and-bolts resource to help adults nurture the faith and lives of emerging generations. I want to help you strategically apply a biblical theology of ministry to *in-betweens*, young people who are no longer children but not yet adults. The idea behind *Adoptive Church* is that any church or organization can embrace an adoptive ministry model that will help young people and others experience full inclusion in the body of Christ.

You can play a significant role in leading your church or group toward an adoptive model that creates the kind of community and relational atmosphere where young people can live into their mutual adoption into God's family. I will show you how to navigate these waters while also seeking leadership buy-in. One essential for your journey is a solid grounding in the three core competencies required to move your group or congregation closer to an adoptive model.

(I believe these are essentials for *any* church that seeks to function as a Christ-centered body, but they are especially important in creating the kind of environment where members of God's family of all ages can thrive together.)

The three core competencies for developing an adoptive church ministry are the following:

1. Pursuing intentional community
2. Living in service on behalf of one another
3. Welcoming the outsider

Pursuing Intentional Community (Ephesians 4:16)

There are only a few places in the Gospels when Jesus says, "Pay attention, I mean this one. Write it down, talk about it, and make sure this is at the forefront of everything you do." When he does, it deserves special notice. In John 15:1–17, on the night before he was killed, Jesus gave one of these talks to his friends and disciples. "I am the vine; you are the branches," he said, reminding me that I am not to live on my own as an individual branch, but I am to hang out with my fellow branches.

Then in verse 12, and again in verse 17, he tells us, "This is my command: Love each other." These were among the last direct words Jesus said to his closest friends hours before being killed. The importance of this new command, especially at this final hour, cannot be overstated. Jesus's command to love each other is at the heart of his mission and message.

In Ephesians 4:16, Paul reminds the gathered followers of Jesus that intimate relationships and connectedness is a partnership of the work of God through the Spirit and the work of the people: "From him the whole body, joined and held together by every supporting ligament, grows and builds itself up in love, as each part does its work." It is God who bonds us together as a household of children, but it is up to each of us to "do our work" as we engage with, listen to, encourage, and support one another. We do our work, and the Holy Spirit does his. That is how we grow.

If you want to build a community that welcomes and receives the young as siblings, there must be a community willing and able to receive them. This is what the youth pastors in the seminar were so concerned about. How can we trust a church that in reality is not all that interested in being a community to offer intentional body life to them? It's simple, really. Without a commitment to pursuing this competency, adoptive youth ministry will remain really tough.

Living in Service on Behalf of One Another (John 13:1–17)

This competency might be a little more difficult for some readers to envision, but it is so clearly biblical that it would seem like every church would at least be talking about it. In all four Gospels, Jesus makes it really clear: we find life when we give it away.

John 13 includes an example of this kind of self-emptying love. In the upper room on the night before his crucifixion, Jesus does the unthinkable. He washes the disciples' feet, even though it was unheard of for an esteemed rabbi to do such a thing. Jesus then does something more mystifying: he tells the disciples to do for each other what he has done for them. By instructing them to wash one another's feet, Jesus establishes a permanent bond between humility and leadership. This bond should be evident in Jesus's followers for all time.

Today when we wash feet, it is often so symbolic that it might not mean much. But when we have the attitude of ancient foot washers, when we are willing to take up the towel, get on our knees, and offer our service on behalf of someone else, then we are living into what Jesus told his friends that night.

If a church acknowledges that service is its basic posture, and members practice sacrificial hospitality toward one another and the world at large, adoptive youth ministry will be a natural fit. But if a church is less familial and more private or divided into subgroups, adoptive ministry may have a hard time taking hold.

Welcoming the Outsider (Hebrews 13:2)

When you carefully study the life of Jesus and look for new insights into who he was on earth, it's tough to miss how he treated the broken, the failed, the outcast, the outsider.

Every time he encountered someone who could be considered vulnerable, he was tender and gentle in his dealings with them. He was only harsh with those who should know better, such as his disciples and the religious leaders.

Consider Jesus's encounter with the woman at the well in John 4. When he asks her to go call her husband, knowing full well that she had had five husbands and was living with another man currently, Jesus knew that the timing of this encounter had given him the space to enter her world in this way. He demonstrated even there that his intentions were kind, not condemning, because the woman not only stayed but also engaged more deeply with him. Jesus was consistently hospitable to the vulnerable.

Openness to outsiders is a core part of what it means to be a Christ-centered community. As Hebrews 13:2 puts it, "Do not forget to show hospitality to strangers, for by so doing some people have shown hospitality to angels without knowing it."

If a congregation is seriously grappling with how it can relate to those who feel neglected or "outside," there's a good chance young people may feel they're wanted and loved. Being welcoming is a way of developing the spiritual practice of hospitality. This can be a sign to young people that they're approaching a family they can relate to and be a part of.

But don't bother pretending to be welcoming if you're not really committed. Young people can smell a superficial hello a mile away. They know the difference between "forty-five seconds of friendly" and a true invitation to relationship.

This issue comes up frequently in youth ministry. Churches that have a mission statement that shouts "All are welcome" sometimes can get a little nervous when neighborhood kids whose parents want nothing to do with the church take over the middle school program. Yet, if church leaders are willing to address our easily conflicting values of wanting the best for "our own kids" while also knowing the importance of being a welcoming community to outsiders, then adoptive youth ministry can be a great catalyst for deeper exploration of how to address that conflict.

Including students as fully invested and celebrated participants in the full life of God's household is the ultimate test of how deeply a church is willing to go to make sure that the community functions as a family of siblings. This is where *Adoptive Church* veers from the last four or five decades of youth ministry history.

We can no longer "do" youth ministry. We must live as the church, the family of God. Youth ministry that focuses only on students and neglects the larger body is not a fully biblical youth ministry. It's youth work in a Christian cultural setting.

When God brought us into his family, he didn't give us the option of disconnecting ourselves from one another. We can't really call ourselves members of the church of Jesus Christ if that's our attitude. In Christ, you and I are adopted siblings in God's household, and we belong to each other, whether we feel vulnerable or dominant. This is the foundational premise of adoptive youth ministry.

PART ONE

The Goal of an Adoptive Church

If you want to take the first step in practicing adoptive youth ministry in order to create an adoptive church, you need to know where you want to end up.

In a sport, it's a winning game or season. In a play or a film, it's how the hero learns something new. In getting an education, it's walking across that stage, diploma in hand. In adoptive youth ministry, it is helping each and every young person find their place as a faithful follower of Jesus Christ and live as a specifically called agent in the mission of God alongside the family of believers. This is what an adoptive church is committed to, and therefore the goal of any adoptive ministry. This is the ultimate goal of adoptive youth ministry.

But what is unique about *adoptive* youth ministry? Doesn't the goal stated above sound pretty much like every other vision statement for youth ministry you've ever heard? There are some similarities. An adoptive church emphasizes helping young people navigate the complexities of life and faith as they mature. It acknowledges that adolescents need a dedicated time and space to feel safe while exploring the gospel. And it acknowledges that adults can play a big role in guiding young people toward connections within the larger faith community. So far, so good.

What sets an adoptive church apart is twofold:

- *Strategy*. Everything we do is shaped by the end we have in mind—full integration into Christ's body. That desired outcome or goal drives our thinking, our strategy, and our programming.
- *Lens*. Everything we do is driven by our perspective. We view everything—evangelism, discipleship, leadership, and relationships within the body—through the lens of the household of God.

You've heard the saying "If you aim at nothing, you'll hit it every time." How many times have we seen this in youth work?

Adoptive youth ministry helps us refine our goals. Everything we do is in the service of who we are in Christ. Once orphaned by the fall of humanity, all who are in Christ are granted the "power" to become children of God. That means every mission trip we take and every small group we run is designed around the future of that one student in relationship to the church. That is what makes adoptive ministry compelling.

In part 1 of this book we begin the process of creating an adoptive youth ministry by defining the role and the goal of our adoptive life together. This section presents the why and what of adoptive youth ministry.

We start with the reason for adoptive youth ministry, then examine the role and the goal of adoptive youth ministry, and conclude with a basic theology and praxis of what an adopted disciple of Christ looks like. This section will provide the groundwork for forming an adoptive church in any setting regardless of tradition or denomination or whether you are rural, suburban, urban, or international.

Because adoptive youth ministry is not so much a model as a way of thinking and living as a community, this book will help you apply these ideas on the outskirts of Chicago, in rural Ontario, or even in Nairobi.

We are the body of Christ, we have been adopted in Christ into God's household, and the day has come when the church is beginning to see that young people are invaluable in strengthening its health and vitality. The goal of adoptive youth ministry is that every child, every adolescent, and every emerging adult will find their way home through the nurturing love and active empowerment of the body of Christ.

2

Adoptive Youth Ministry

FROM ME TO US

Youth ministry has been around since at least 1844, when England's Young Men's Christian Association was formed to provide urban youth with positive alternatives to the sins of the city. American youth ministry really took off in the 1930s and 1940s, and pretty much ever since we youth workers have been following the same programmatic model.

For decades, the focus of the programmatic youth ministry model has been crystal clear: creating and leading programs. The youth leader's main job is to run events and classes designed to "graduate" students who are mature in their faith.

But if you look around churches today, or talk to men and women who lead youth ministries, it's clear that the old programmatic model isn't working like it used to. The youth ministry machine simply isn't generating the graduates it once did.

There are many reasons the programmatic model is failing. For one, growing up has changed so much in our culture that the ways we reach out and communicate the gospel to young people are no longer producing the outcomes we seek. There is also increasing awareness that authentic, long-term spiritual transformation is not so easily programmable. Spiritual growth is a lengthy, messy process that demands more today than what we have been offering.

Don't get me wrong. No movement dies off quickly. The programmatic model goes on as usual in many places and can even be a viable, if not vibrant, expression of ministry. Yet, inevitably, when we rely on programs and events to literally be the sum total of our ministry, our efforts eventually become more about the machine of our program and not about the people we serve. In either case, whether we are seeing a programmatic approach diminish in ministry effectiveness or we hold on to former ways of doing the church, whenever something new and enticing comes along (whether a book, a tweaked "model," or a popular speaker or musician) our default response is to dust off the old approaches and hope they will work this time.

The sky is not falling, because many students enjoy events, annual trips, and even the regular youth gatherings. It's still possible to keep the old machine going with enough resources—solid leadership, a good facility, shared history, and momentum. And there will always be the superstar kids with spectacular stories that we can point to and claim as our results. "Youth ministry still works!" we say.

One thing hasn't changed. Everyone involved in youth ministry wants to see young people come to a sincere, integrated, mature faith in Jesus Christ that is expressed in love for God, neighbor, and self. That goal has not changed. But *how* we go about reaching the goal has changed drastically because we realize we are missing so many kids, including even those who were raised in the church. This is more than an academic debate. It's about the lives and destinies of the next generation. The clock is ticking for our students and us. What can we do?

Adopted into God's Family

While the programmatic model relies on events where we can tell kids God's story, adoptive youth ministry seeks *to show young people that their calling and destiny is located not only in God's story but among God's people living out that story.*

Many youth workers tap into the parachurch youth ministry world, but let's look at youth ministry through the lens of the church. If we are honest with ourselves, most of us will admit that the long history of youth ministry has created two-plus generations of spiritual orphans who attend youth ministry events regularly but gradually show less and less commitment to the church, the gathered body of Christ. Once they graduate from high school and the youth ministry programming, many also graduate from church.

This has gone on too long for us to miss it or pretend it doesn't happen. This has led me to ask an important question: What if we designed youth ministry with the end in mind? If our goal is growing the church and seeing young people grafted into this larger community of faith, what might we do to help our students reach that goal?

I actually tried to answer these questions in two earlier books: *Starting Right: Thinking Theologically about Youth Ministry*[1] and *Four Views of Youth Ministry and the Church*.[2] In my contributions to both books, I argue that the goal of youth ministry should be developing kids' loyalty to and involvement in the church, but I hadn't quite figured out a theological or even practical way to make this happen.[3] In the last few years, many have begun to explore a more church-focused approach to youth ministry, what I call adoptive youth ministry, but across the youth ministry spectrum the program-centered way of serving young people remains the default.

Three Crises Facing Youth Ministry Today

If books do not convince people, perhaps circumstances will. I've noticed more and more youth ministry leaders acknowledging that the old model isn't working. Here are three issues that should concern us.

First, we are losing kids at an alarming rate.[4]

Second, our world is becoming increasingly secularized, presenting challenges to students that may not reveal themselves until these young people are far beyond our reach.

Third, while we have known for some time that kids are hurting, many leaders now acknowledge that there's more hurt out there than we realized. Growing up today takes its toll on every teenager, not just those we consider "at risk."

Let's take a closer look at these three crises.

Numbers and Nones: We're Losing Our Students

What's the fastest-growing "religious" group in America today? It's the *nones*: those with no religious preference or affiliation.

In 2011 the Fuller Youth Institute (FYI) launched the Sticky Faith series of books, articles, training, website, and curriculum.[5] I co-authored the initial *Sticky Faith* volume with Kara Powell, executive director of FYI. Our subtitle spelled out the book's goal: *Everyday Ideas to Build Lasting Faith in Your Kids.*[6]

Sticky Faith was based on research into what makes faith last. Fuller Seminary initiated its College Transition Project to explore the state of young adults' faith after high school. The findings showed that "40–50 percent of kids who graduate from a church or youth group will fail to stick with their faith in college."[7] (I also addressed "sticky" issues in *Hurt 2.0: Inside the World of Today's Teenagers.*)[8]

Sticky Faith quickly became a major influence in youth ministry. It was not only the most widely cited research into the actual reality of adolescents' long-term faith; it also confirmed what we had suspected for some time: for all the good that youth ministry has done and is doing, too many students fail to stick around through graduation.

In 2012 a team of Canadian researchers studied youth "stickiness" in their country. The study, "Hemorrhaging Faith: Why and When Canadian Young Adults Are Leaving, Staying and Returning to Church," was sobering.[9] John Wilkinson of the Evangelical Fellowship of Canada shared three key findings:

- Only one in three Canadian young adults who attended church weekly as a child still does so today.
- Of the young adults who no longer attend church, half have also stopped identifying themselves with the Christian tradition in which they were raised.
- Four primary toxins keep young people from engaging with the church: hypocrisy, judgment, exclusivity, and failure.

Study after study has removed all doubt: we now know that we are losing at least half of our kids, including even some of the most committed.

Culture Clash: Students Unprepared for a Secular Society

Allison, who approached me at a recent youth ministry convention, is one of these lost ones, as I learned while listening to her story:

I'm not the kind of person who ever thought I would be in this situation, because my Christian experience was so good. My parents sincerely loved God and their kids, and our home was actually pretty healthy, compared to some of the homes I've seen.

My parents were deeply invested in church, and that was always a very positive thing for me. I embraced their faith and made it my own. I became active myself, and also got involved with national youth ministries. I went to a good Christian college where real thought was encouraged. And unlike other students I knew, my faith never wavered.

After college I went into "full-time Christian service" [gestures with fingers to create quotation marks] on the staff of a parachurch youth ministry organization. Those first years were magical in every way. It was like I had been designed to do this work, and I quickly climbed the ladder into more responsible leadership positions. Everything was great.

Then suddenly, it wasn't. Two years into the work, it was like something was shifting in me, and the very things that had been so fulfilling and affirming and life-giving to me suddenly became chores I had to do as part of my job.

I felt like I was in a holding pattern. I was stuck in my job, but I didn't feel the passion anymore. That's pretty much when I quit going to church. I didn't really get much out of it, and no one there really connected with me.

My parents didn't really pick up on what was going on because whenever we talked about faith, it was always about doing ministry, not anything personal. I didn't feel I could talk to anybody about what was going on, until I met Jeremy.

He's the kindest, smartest, most fun person I've ever met. He makes me feel alive in a way I've never felt before. One thing I love is he's a seeker, you know? He doesn't have it all figured out, chapter and verse. He's helped me see that everything I've always believed about Jesus is less about God, really, than it is about me lending my support to a centuries-old cultural myth that perpetuates white, male, Protestant control.

Chap, the way I see God has changed. For me, it's more about love than which church you go to, and honestly, I feel kind of deceived by my parents and my church.

Allison wasn't asking me to help her figure out God, or her relationship with Jeremy. She wanted me to help her figure out how to maintain her job, relationships, and current lifestyle now that Christ was receding into the background of her life.

My heart was breaking too much to come up with anything good to say. I was saddened when Allison said nobody at work had noticed anything different in her spiritual life or work performance, even though her heart wasn't in it anymore.

That's when the light went on for me, as it had so many times in previous conversations. It wasn't college or Jeremy that had convinced Allison that church was largely irrelevant. Parachurch youth ministry organizations, for the most part, can ignore the value of connecting to a local congregation, or at least implicitly communicate that a church is less than necessary for a young disciple. In this case, since middle school, Allison had not been led to consider the church as her family.

Once Allison had some distance from the cultural Christian "bubble" that she had lived within most of her life, her worldview began to open up. Working in a ministry allowed her to maintain a Christian identity for a season. But as she began to broaden her relationships outside of her work and faith community, she encountered a whole new world she had never considered before. Her story is perhaps not so much that she *lost* her faith as she *adjusted* her faith to adapt to the new world she encountered—a new world that none of the various Christian influences in her life successfully prepared her to face.

As time went on, she eventually left the faith of her family and ministry behind.

Sadly, she's not alone.

Under Pressure: Hurting and All Alone

I write and talk so much about the hurt at the heart of so many young people that some people dismiss me as "the king of pain." But a growing body of research shows that today's students feel they are under intense pressure to perform to the agendas and expectations of an increasingly impersonal and disconnected world.

Their sense of isolation, pain, and struggle is often combined with an absence of positive social support, leaving many feeling like they're totally on their own to navigate the rapidly changing social environment. Depending on personalities and circumstances, young people can feel vulnerable, deeply bruised, angry, and intensely isolated.[10]

David Elkind portrays the pressure kids face: "Today's child has become the unwilling, unintended victim of overwhelming stress—the stress borne of rapid, bewildering social change and constantly rising expectations."[11]

When you grow up in an atomized, individualized society filled with agendas, worldviews, intense social-media competition, and little or no adult support, no wonder it feels like you're living inside a pressure cooker. The prospect of journeying into mature, adjusted adulthood seems like a sick joke or, for some, a brutal death march.

The living gospel of Christ embodied in the company of the faithful has power to confront these pressures, but too many young people eventually find that the individualistic faith they embraced when they made a personal "decision" for Christ doesn't provide a strong enough foundation to stand on when they face the realities of life in the world.

I know that people make fun of the millennial generation, but I do not join them. It's a big world out there, and I'm not sure that all the youth ministry programs and special events really prepare them to survive and thrive in the world they will soon inhabit.

I'm not saying we need to blow the whole thing up. Camps and mission trips continue to change lives. Students engaged in leadership opportunities still seem to grow and mature into Christ-centered leaders. Organizations like Young Life have a solid track record of bringing young people to Christ in middle school and high school.

Yet they know that once a student graduates, if they haven't been connected to a local church, there is a great probability that many of their most devoted attendees will abandon their faith. I am saying that the crises young people face today reveal the crises in our historical approach to youth ministry. The programmatic approach, which, even when done well, seems to form young people who believe that Christianity is something that belongs solely to me, is ultimately isolating and individualized. As one friend (who has chosen to remain anonymous) wrote to me in response to this chapter, "Faith is more about the youth group schedule of events than it is about growing and challenging relationships, resulting in the crisis that when kids are stripped of the program they became used to, they experience a stripping of meaning and purpose to the faith. They actually walk away with no 'internal sense of meaning' because it's all been resting on external programs."

I believe there's a better way. Instead of sending young people out into the world on their own, let's introduce them to a powerful resource that's bigger and stronger than their own internal sense of meaning: their family of faith in the universal body of Christ.

I Was Wrong: A Theological Reflection on Youth Ministry in the Church

If it sounds like I'm preaching to you, you're right. But I'm also preaching to myself. When I talk about leaders who have emphasized youth ministry at the expense of the church, I must plead guilty.

For years I've argued that those who do youth ministry should *advocate* for youth ministry. That's why I have written, taught, and spoken on the value of youth ministry, the need for youth ministry, and the church's culpability in not empowering a greater emphasis on youth ministry.

I've pretty much looked at *all* ministry through the lens of youth ministry, and that's where I made my fundamental error. My mistake was to insist—without biblical support or historical evidence— that youth ministry was the most important kind of ministry in the church. And if anybody disagreed with me, I accused them of not really caring about kids as I did.

Now, instead of trying to separate out my personal favorite population from the Christian faith community and focusing only on that subgroup, I'm trying to focus more broadly. I want to see ministry the way Christ sees it: whole.

For too long, too many of us have looked only at our piece of the puzzle, not the whole puzzle. May God heal our ecclesiological blindness!

Strengthen What's Broken

Youth ministry is not dead, nor is it irrelevant. But it's broken, and we need to do what we can to fix it.

We can start by investing more energy thinking ecclesiologically than we do thinking programmatically. The question isn't, What am I going to do next Sunday morning? It's, What am I doing today to connect my students to all the other people in this congregation who are ready and willing to love and care for them?

Instead of standing apart from the church and criticizing it for not caring enough, I'm going to move closer and take youth ministry in their direction. Instead of seeing youth ministry as something that's outside the church body, I want to see the body in the fullness of its gifts for ministering to today's children, adolescents, and emerging adults. As we lead young people to faith in Christ, let's also usher them into a vibrant relationship with Christ's body.

It's not enough to invite kids to faith and to discipleship if we do not encourage and equip them to find themselves as part of God's household through history. Adoptive youth ministry challenges all of us to see how youth ministry fits into this story. And for that, I thank God.

3

Creating Environments Where Faith Families Flourish

When I ask youth workers about the goals of youth ministry, most respond in one of two ways:

- *Doers* focus on action: organizing activities, carrying out programs, and scheduling big events like mission trips so students will learn about the Bible and Christian living.
- *Disciple makers* focus on Christ's "Great Commission" (although he didn't call it that) at the end of Matthew. For them, it's about bringing young people to the point where they accept Christ as their personal Savior.

But then when I ask youth workers to tell me how their stated goals align with how they actually run their ministries, I receive fewer confident responses. I have found that too many youth workers simply don't give much thought to connecting the dots between their youth ministry practices and the results and outcomes they say they desire.

Many doers embrace what I call the *youth ministry machine*—the network of churches, parachurch organizations, conferences, blog posts, and publishers that pump out a steady stream of ready-to-use programs and materials. Created by experts and talented designers, these resources are designed for a youth pastor's immediate use without any personal reflection or preparation.

I confess, my generation of leaders is largely responsible for this model. Once upon a time, there was no such thing as youth ministry. Young people simply tried to involve themselves in adult church programming.

But then a bunch of us young rebels rose up and declared, "Young people deserve their own form of ministry." (This trend was happening not just in youth ministry but in education, youth sports, and many other ways adults tried to help young people flourish.) We tried many new exercises and activities with young people, and when one of them "worked," we passed this activity around in our networks so others could do the same activity with their kids. In time, our networks became parachurch organizations and publishers that promoted ready-to-use activities and programs.

Perhaps unintentionally we sold a generation of youth workers on the idea that youth ministry equals doing such activities and programs, that little more is required. If you follow what some call "best practices," you're good to go.

Resources are great tools, but when we mistake tools for goals, we get lost. We can wind up thinking we are being successful if we simply offer kids a nonstop conveyor belt of goodies and the kids actually show up.

The assumption is that so long as kids attend, participate, say the right things, and behave well in groups, they must be solid followers of Jesus. When we see a ninth grader coming to youth group every week, actively taking part in a small group, going to church with her parents, and seeming sincere in "pursuing her faith," doers feel that their work is done.

The disciple-maker model has its own goals. At the core of many evangelical Christian youth ministries is the desire to help lead John or Joan toward a personal knowledge of and commitment to faith in

Christ that lasts a lifetime. Youth workers "stand in the gap" between Christ and today's generation of teens. You can find this goal clearly stated in many books, convention talks, and blog posts: individual salvation and discipleship for individual believers. When kids truly know and have a relationship with Christ, disciple makers feel our work is done.

If only everything were so easy. As we've seen in recent years, the fastest-growing "religious" group in America is the nonreligious: nones who profess no religious affiliation.[1] The ranks of the nones are full of the Johns and Joans who used to be in our youth groups but have since graduated from both our group and their Christian "phase."

All our plans and good intentions, small groups and mission trips do not necessarily produce the graduates and outcomes we pray for. Trips can release young people from the pretense and burdens of the everyday and ordinary. Missions and service opportunities can help them to see outside and beyond themselves. Small groups can teach them empathy and till the emotional soil for a willingness and ability to go deep with others as they move through life.

All great stuff! The problem isn't, and hasn't ever been, "youth ministry." The problem is twofold: the theological weakness of our "goal" and the inability to be strategic in pursuit of that goal. Ministry is far less about what we *do* and much more about *where we are going.* That's why goals are the essence of adoptive youth ministry.

The Point of Adoptive Youth Ministry: A Growing Family

The point of adoptive youth ministry is to help young people see that by faith in Christ they are part of a new family. Our role in this is to create an environment and employ strategies that will not only introduce adolescents and emerging adults to faith in Jesus Christ but also help them live out that faith as participants and contributors to the family of God.

I don't want to see any more young people go through our ministries, with all their activities and decisions for Christ, and graduate feeling disconnected from both Christ and the family of God.

Again, the gift (or "right" in John 1:12) of the incarnation is to be drawn into a new reality as siblings in God's household. Certainly we will do activities. Certainly we will lead our students into a deeper connection and commitment to Christ. But adoptive youth ministry calls us to come alongside young people in the name and with the compassion of God so that in Christ they move from being lost to being found. As they encounter and consider the call of the good news, they will see that it is fulfilled in community. No one is created or designed to be alone (Gen. 2:18).

This is the core message of adoptive youth ministry: God has provided young people not only with an eternal way home but also with a family right here in the world where, by faith in Jesus, they can experience now what it means to be a beloved sibling in God's household. This is the reason we do everything we do.

Families thrive in healthy environments. Let's see how you can create the kind of environment where members of God's family can thrive.

Three Keys to Creating an Adoptive Environment

Being a Christian means more than having fire insurance against hell and the promise of eternal life later on. Knowing Christ means experiencing an intimate and authentic family-like connection with the household of God right now.

I can hear some of the activity-obsessed doers complaining, "Chap, that sounds so out of touch . . . b-o-r-i-n-g." Perhaps the doubters have never seen what I've witnessed.

It's amazing to see the transformation in young people who are jaded by a world where adults don't really care for them, have been rejected by a world where they don't fit in, or have been judged by a world where all that matters are performance and conformity.

When young people get a chance to experience Christian community through deep intergenerational relationships and shared core values, they latch on to it for all they're worth.

I've had kids tell me about a lifetime of being shamed while playing sports, or of being forced to embrace an all-pleasing image that they know is not them, or of teachers, neighbors, and parents who never say "I love you" without attaching a demand: "Have you finished your report yet? Have you cleaned up your room yet?"

Many teenagers and young adults have an innate distrust of adult power and authority. That's because they've witnessed and experienced its abuse throughout their lives. Why should they trust the church, one of the most powerful bastions of adult power? Why must being a Christian require me to submit myself to a bunch of adults I don't know?

For the gospel to take root in the lives of young people, we need to start by making them welcome in our midst. I'm not talking about welcome as a passive verb, where you sit back and wait for someone to seek your group. I'm talking about welcome as an active verb, where you invest the energy and effort to invite one and all to Christ's big family banquet. We need to actively communicate to each and every precious young person God grants us the chance to lead: "We want you here. We will make room for you. We will weave you into this family."

We have to be the initiators of welcome and inclusion. We have to take the lead. We take the first step. We must be willing to stretch out and bridge the often uncomfortable chasm between one person and another.

I believe that if we are to be effective in adoptive ministry, we must let go of any notions that the focus of our youth ministry should be on reaching and celebrating only the top jocks, the elite students, the extreme extroverts, and the key influencers. These students already have their rewards, and while they of course need our care and attention, it must not be at the expense of anyone else.

I believe authentic ministry must follow the model Jesus set when he was incarnated among us: protecting the vulnerable, embracing the outcast, recognizing the neglected, and healing the broken.

Youth workers who follow the doer and the disciple-maker models need to follow the practical advice that Dr. Kara Powell, executive director of the Fuller Youth Institute, offered in an interview with *Christianity Today*: "View your church through the eyes of a young person."[2]

When you see church from their vantage point, you can see why a genuine, vibrant community that loves and values them is so precious and unique. Such a community can help them navigate the three development tasks of adolescence and emerging adulthood: the development of identity, owning an internal locus of control and autonomy, and having a place to belong that is bigger than themselves.

There are three keys to creating an environment of welcome and inclusion:

1. Nurturing young people
2. Empowering young people
3. Including young people

Nurturing Young People

When I am invited to preach or speak, I typically rent a car so that after I've given folks everything, I can go somewhere—either to a hotel hot tub or a small gathering with friends—where I don't have to preach or speak anymore.

But having access to a car keeps me from encounters like the one I had with a pastor who insisted on taking me to the airport himself.

"I liked your adoptive ministry talk," he told me. "Now I get what my sixteen-year-old son needs. I've got to get five men to pour into his life."

As he drove, he catalogued his many complaints about his son. He was a disappointment. He just needed to grow up and to learn how to be a man for a change.

"That's why I need to find five great men who can pour themselves into him and show him what it means to be a man of God."

Yellow and red flags started to fly in my mind.

For one thing, while I believe that young people would appreciate a few adult men and women to gently and organically come alongside and care for them, I'm not sure the way to achieve this is by having a father finding other like-minded guys to "pour into him."

As common as it is, the "pouring" language does not reflect what adoptive ministry looks like. I know it's popular lingo, but doesn't pouring usually mean one person is a big pitcher full of water and the other person is an empty vessel? Even when lovingly applied, this approach can be one-way and top-down. Adoptive youth ministry is more about providing support and care to a young person than it is about pouring. As Paul puts it to his friends in Thessalonica, "For you know that we dealt with each of you as a father deals with his own children, encouraging, comforting and urging you to live lives worthy of God" (1 Thess. 2:11–12). And even that word, *urging*, is not with the intensity of "pouring into" but the offering of hope. That's what the five adults in the life of a young person represent—not a one-way directing, but a mutual and organic friendship that an adult sibling offers.

The concept of nurture comes from the Latin "to suckle, to nourish" and later "the act of nursing."[3] In English, to nurture means to "care for and protect (someone or something) while they are growing."[4] Let's explore how adoptive ministries can nurture the young by both protecting and caring for them.

I know many ministries that seek to protect and care for young people. Some are very effective. But what happens when kids graduate and leave your program? Will they continue to live well and engage the world in ways that strengthen their life and their faith? Will they continue to live into their mutual adoption as siblings in the household of God?

Protection means more than permission slips and health forms and adequate supervision on trips and at lock-ins. These are important, but God's family can also protect young people's developing hearts and psyches. We can help young people interpret and filter the world they encounter so they know how to respond. That may mean providing them with resources and experts when it comes to issues of gender discrimination, violence, media, and the like. It also means being present enough with them so that we adults are able to more deeply understand what it is like to be a young person in this culture. This understanding would allow us to engage with them as they move through adolescence.

How to explain caring? I believe compassion is key. Henri Nouwen said that to show compassion means "to suffer with" another.[5] This is loving with teeth. Instead of building a wall of protection around our young, or hiring the best staff to lead them, an adoptive community comes alongside the young and "suffers with" each one.

To suffer with others, we must initiate relationships with them. We must seek to know them and know about them. We must do what is not done by anyone else in their world: we must commit to remaining close by every person God brings into our church families. We must embody sacrificial love and compassion to truly nurture these others. Practically, caring with compassion means we must:

- demonstrate our compassion so we can build bridges of trust;
- actively show respect for each person instead of waiting for them to show respect to us;
- listen to them instead of trying to force them to listen to us;
- initiate relationships without pushing our agenda or timetable on them;
- seek to empathize with them, meaning we sit on the steps of their world, making sure that they know that we are interested in what their life is like; and
- advise and share *only when asked*, knowing that when they are ready and trust us, we are most able to speak in a way that encourages and builds them up.

By following these practical principles of caring with compassion, we heed Paul's admonishment in Colossians 4:5: "Be wise in the way you act toward outsiders; make the most of every opportunity."

Empowering Young People

How many times have you heard someone say, "Young people are the future of the church"? Many times when I've heard it, the unsubtle message is that adults get to control things for now, and the young people can take over once we're all dead.

When it comes to their faith, every young person needs to know that they have value as siblings in the household of God. All too often, even in youth ministry, we have limited empowerment to serving the internal youth ministry program or succumbed to a church's plea for warm bodies to "teach" in the children's ministry. Occasionally, a church may require a special ability, and because there is no one else who can fill that need, a church may seek out (and call it "empower") a student to serve (like a bass player for the worship band, or someone to help usher or park cars). Under these circumstances, a young person who is given the opportunity to contribute may or may not feel a sense of empowerment in the process. When a task is offered without a commitment to proactively naming that student's worth and value as a member of the adoptive community, they intuitively know that they are simply filling a need. In these circumstances, they rarely feel a sense of authentic empowerment. Yet when a belief in the contribution of a young person is celebrated and affirmed in the faith community, *in recognition of their importance to that body*, their sense of self and ability to make a difference strengthens their sense of worth and connection to the broader community. This is empowerment. Here are three ways we can empower young people.

Involve the Whole Community

Communicating to students that they are valuable needs to happen outside the walls and networks of the youth ministry. They need to be welcome participants in the whole community.

An adoptive church looks to avoid a scenario where a high school student may be valued as a third-grade Sunday school teacher, but her value reaches only as far as the children's ministry staff. Nor would this church be content with a situation where a sound tech played an integral part of the production staff, but no one outside the department even knows what he does or who he is.

To intentionally empower the young to feel like they are important members of the church family, we must find creative and strategic ways for them to be seen and celebrated as vital to the household of faith. To do that, we need lots of adults to know every young person who calls our church their home.

Become "Keychain Leaders"

According to Kara Powell, Jake Mulder, and Brad Griffin, "keychain leaders" are leaders who "are acutely aware of the keys on their keychain and intentional about entrusting and empowering all generations, including teenagers and emerging adults, with their own set of keys."[6]

The idea is not to just hand off keys to young people, letting them simply take over a ministry or event. Keychain leaders are strategic, present, and involved. They want to empower young people to discover and use their gifts to contribute to and participate in the life and work of the community, whatever it takes. This can take a myriad of forms, but the common commitment is that, in as many ways and avenues as it takes, every teenager and young adult needs to be able to engage their God-given leadership in a way that embodies their value and place.

Help Young People Develop Their Gifts and Callings

One of the more prominent struggles of church ministry is what staff tend to call "recruiting volunteers." In the body of Christ, the leadership's job is not to "recruit" anybody to any task. Rather, it is our role to empower the laity to participate in and contribute to the household of faith.

As Paul puts it, our job is "to equip his people for works of service, so the body of Christ may be built up" (Eph. 4:12). When we recruit people to a specific task, or even label or slot people according to a programmatic need we have identified, loyalty is rarely built.

When it comes to empowering young people, don't just use them as a form of plug and play. Don't automatically squeeze them into your mold, but work with them to see how the Spirit is working in their lives to grow their gifts.

Ask them what drew them to serve and what they hope to contribute by serving. Using these insights, work together to develop a job description that both contributes to the needs of the community and empowers the young person's need to know that they matter.

Including Young People

How do we include the young in ways that help them feel like they are genuine and necessary parts of the whole community? This is about both attitude and intentionality. Do you truly *want* to invite young people to participate? How seriously do the leaders and the adults in your community take the contributions of the young in the business of the whole? These are the questions to ask ourselves.

It is also up to us, as adults and as ministry leaders, to make sure that we are not just *talking* about inviting the young into the life and work of our Christian body but actually making that happen. This can include everything from their serving in a coleadership role to being on a leadership advisory team. If you offer adult education as well as youth ministry, you can put the normal age-segregated programming on hold maybe two or three times a year and offer elective classes that draw high school students and adults into dialogue. During the Academy Awards season, for example, one Southern California church offers a six-week series on some of the movies up for Best Picture, and everyone (including teenagers) is welcome. They watch assigned films and then gather weekly to discuss the theological and cultural content of the film. The dialogue is livelier than it would be with only adults!

Adoptive ministry is for all of us—not just the clergy or staff, but the entire community—to commit to creating a church-wide environment where the young know that they matter.

4

Making Disciples among Siblings

THE ADOPTIVE PROCESS OF CHRISTIAN FORMATION

True character transformation begins, we are taught to believe, in the pure grace of God and is continually assisted by it. Very well. But *action* is also indispensable in making the Christian truly a different kind of person. . . . Failure to act in certain definite ways will guarantee that this transformation does not come to pass.

—Dallas Willard, *Spirit of the Disciplines*[1]

o and make disciples of all nations," Jesus told his followers before he ascended into heaven (Matt. 28:19). Ever since then, for twenty centuries, this Great Commission has been the primary task of the church.

Jesus has commanded those of us who follow him to *go* and make *more* Christ followers. As Dallas Willard makes clear above, we must *act* to fulfill that command.

In Western Christian circles over the last half century, making disciples has largely meant evangelizing *individuals* so they make *individual* decisions to follow Christ. Adoptive ministry takes a more communitarian approach to fulfilling Christ's command. Yes, making a disciple means introducing someone to Christ. Yes, making a disciple means teaching them what it means to live as a disciple. But disciple making can't stop there.

Adoptive ministry says our commission is not accomplished until we place these Christ followers within a committed Christian community. Our mission doesn't stop with helping a person connect with Christ. We must also help them connect deeply to Christ's family here on earth. That is the heart of adoptive youth ministry.

It seems many youth workers have uncritically absorbed an individualistic approach to disciple making. This chapter will help you explore what it means to make disciples who experience adoption into the Christian family.

Worried Frank and Me

Frank, a forty-something-year-old volunteer counselor who had just completed a week at a Christian camp, was agitated because of my teaching.

"I've never heard anything like that before," he said. "All this about 'trusting in Jesus'? Is that it?"

Frank was talking to me as hundreds of campers were fleeing the camp's large meeting hall to jump in to the vans and buses that would transport them back home. He and I had talked often during the week, but he wasn't sure he liked the way I handled a passage from the book of Acts I had read to the group that night. "[The jailer] brought [Paul and Silas] out and asked, 'Sirs, what must I do to be saved?' They replied, 'Believe in the Lord Jesus, and you will be saved—you and your household'" (Acts 16:30–31).

"You told those kids all they needed to do was *believe*," he said, emphasizing and stretching out the last word. Frank was worried that

I was letting his kids off the hook too easily. Isn't working out our salvation often a difficult struggle (Phil. 2:12)? I acknowledged his point but held my ground. Yes, the Christian life is often a struggle, but God's invitation is still loaded into one word: believe.

"What about obedience?" he asked.

"It follows trust," I said. "It is the response of trust. But trusting comes first."

"I guess I can see that obedience is one way I put trust into action," Frank said. "That sounds good. I can see that I need to encourage their belief and trust in Christ. Okay then, what can I do to disciple our kids better so they trust Jesus more deeply?"

Frank, I appreciate your question! This chapter is for anyone like Frank who practices disciple making among kids and wants to help young people live out their love for Jesus Christ in ways that last a lifetime.

An adoptive church is first and always about believing, or trusting, in Jesus Christ. We learn obedience because we have decided to trust. That is the core of the discipleship message. Here's what we need to do to practice disciple making in an adoptive way.

Trusting Belief in Christ: The Core of Evangelism *and* Discipleship

Adoptive ministry seeks to do what the writer of Hebrews counsels: "Fix your thoughts on Jesus" (Heb. 3:1). There is no other gospel.

For people like Frank, belief is not demanding enough, so they pile on additional behavioral requirements. They tell kids to demonstrate their faith by spending X minutes a day in Bible reading and study and X minutes in prayer. I've seen how kids who grow up in this kind of environment can begin to see meeting these requirements as more important than believing in and loving Christ.

In John 6, Jesus feeds a group of hungry people, who then follow him across a lake, where they finally get to ask him that most fundamental question of faith: "What must we do to do the works that God requires?" (6:28). Jesus gives the same answer to them that Paul and Silas would later give the jailer: "Believe in the one he has sent" (6:29).

Believe. Trust. Have faith.[2] That's the singular message of the gospel, of discipleship, of our adoption through faith into Christ's family.

When the Bible talks about faith, it often describes it as a *process*, not a *thing*. In 2 Thessalonians 1:3 Paul says, "We ought always to thank God for you, brothers and sisters, and rightly so, because your faith is growing more and more." We see similar imagery in Jesus's parable of the sower (Matt. 13:1–23). He describes the word (the seed) being sown in a receptive heart, where it grows.

Certainly discipleship is a process. But as the parable points out, not every seed that's planted successfully makes it through that process. Only the seeds that grow deep roots survive. Trust is the key to the seed being planted in the first place as well as the catalyst for sending down deep roots that lead to mature growth. Adoptive ministry fosters that trust between youth and the sower.[3]

We begin the life of faith through trusting Christ (we call that "repentance," or turning one's life around from trusting ourselves to trusting God).[4] And we continue the process of ongoing repentance by staying the course of trusting Christ. This is our part in the discipleship process. We trust, God transforms.[5]

Returning to the parable of the sower: some seeds landed in poor, rocky soil. That made it tough for them to survive and thrive. Other seeds were planted in good soil, which helped them grow. Adoptive youth ministry focuses on being the good soil, on creating healthy environments where those seeds can grow into fullness and maturity.

But what do terms like *fullness* and *maturity* mean when we're talking about adolescent spiritual development? Let's reexamine what it means to be a disciple of Jesus.

Biblical Discipleship

Everybody has at least a hazy idea of what discipleship means. Let's see if we can remove some of the haze and explore what Christian maturity means, particularly for a thirteen-year-old adolescent or a twenty-five-year-old young adult.

We know that when a person is "in Christ" and has received and trusted in Jesus, she is given the right and the gift to become one of the children of God (John 1:12). Discipleship means helping someone live more deeply into that reality. Maturity is a benchmark that signifies growth.

But growth is so personal, so connected to our individual starting point, our personality, our life journey. What looks like maturity in one person may be gross immaturity in another. Our goal, then, is not a destination that says, "Look, *there's* a mature disciple."[6] It is, rather, a movement and a trajectory toward continual growth. Growth is organic and constant, and we will grow either in one direction (toward deepening trust and faith) or in another (toward greater self-focus and reliance). To disciple someone means to help him grow the deep trust in Christ that will last a lifetime. Adoptive youth ministry is a way to create the environment where that growth can happen in the context of God's household with other siblings on the same journey. That is biblical discipleship.

Jesus began his public ministry as a traveling rabbi, or teacher. He invited people to follow him and become his *disciples*, another word for followers. Scripture teaches that receiving and believing are key to becoming Jesus's disciple and living into our status as adopted children of God. *Receiving* and *believing* are the two most common words used to describe the starting point of the discipled, Christian life.

Some Christians place a premium on people experiencing a specific, identifiable "decision" (as in, "I became a Christian when I was four years old at a Dodgers game with my grandma"). Other Christians aren't so concerned about what happened at one moment in time. They care about what has happened since, and where you are headed tomorrow. They want to know, "Have you oriented your life toward hearing and responding to God's call?"

Every orthodox Christian tradition teaches that followers of Jesus Christ must believe in and follow Christ. Following means growing, because life keeps changing, which in turn challenges us to trust Christ in new and deeper ways. Wherever and however this growth takes place is discipleship.

What Causes Disciples to Grow?

Who does the real work in discipleship: Us? Or God? The New Testament uses two overlapping concepts to describe the work of discipleship and growth:

- We know *we* play a role in our own growth process. We are told we must "work out [our] salvation with fear and trembling" (Phil. 2:12).
- We also know that it is ultimately *God* who transforms us and makes the growth happen, "for it is God who works in you to will and to act in order to fulfill his good purpose" (Phil. 2:13).

Christ's parable of the sower (Matt. 13) shows how these two forces work together—God's transformative work of the Spirit somehow functions with a person's agency. The parable also introduces an important third factor: the soil. That represents the environment where the growth takes place. As we see from the parable, not all soil is equal. Good soil nurtures seeds and fosters growth. Poor soil doesn't have what the seeds need and causes them to wither.

Youth workers who want to be disciplers must focus on soil. Christ's family is that soil. You and I are part of that soil. We need to create the environments where seeds can grow and shoot down deep roots that will last a lifetime. We work as gardeners caring for tender plants who need a healthy environment to deepen their trust in Christ. We can work on preparing a rich garden for the plants God may bring our way by focusing on four things disciples need to experience growth: knowing Christ, loving Christ, following Christ, and trusting Christ.

Knowing Christ

It seems that once Jesus's earliest disciples knew him, they followed him. It has been the same way ever since. The apostle Paul had been in ministry for many years, yet writing from prison, he exclaimed, "I want to know Christ" (Phil. 3:10). Paul also points out that not knowing Christ means we are actually in opposition to him: "They claim to know God, but by their actions they deny him" (Titus 1:16). John makes a similar point: "Whoever does not love does not know God, because God is love" (1 John 4:8).

A. W. Tozer said it well: "It is a well-known law of the spiritual life that our love for God will spring up and flourish just as our knowledge of Him increases. To know Him is to love Him, and to know Him better is to love Him more."[7]

In his *Institutes of the Christian Religion*, John Calvin says divine revelation helps us know and love the one true God: "Scripture, gathering up the otherwise confused knowledge of God in our minds, having dispersed our dullness, clearly shows us the true God."[8]

We teach young disciples about who God is as he is revealed in Scripture, but we don't stop there. We help them *know about* God so they can *know* him personally, as New Testament scholar G. F. Hawthorne suggests: "'To know Christ,' therefore, is the ultimate goal toward which the apostle sets the course of his life. . . . For him the significance of Christ 'in whom are hid all the treasures of wisdom and knowledge' (Col. 2:3) is so vast that even to *begin* to know him is more important than anything else in all the world."[9]

What would it mean for your ministry to focus on helping young people know Christ? In your teaching, in your small groups, in your prayers, and even in your casual conversations with students, you can help them know who Jesus is, both as he is revealed in Scripture and now as he reigns on the throne. Whatever content you have to offer kids is wrapped up in the person, character, words, and work of Jesus; the rest is our response to him. So, for example, spend time framing words or phrases in each of these subcategories (person, character, etc.). Then create a regular ritual in a youth group gathering or small group where you always have a verse and a word or phrase that describes Jesus. Maybe sometimes you talk about it, or maybe you use it to launch into an opening prayer. But keep knowledge of Christ at the forefront of the content you bring to young people.

Loving Christ

When asked to name the greatest commandment, Jesus cited Deuteronomy 6:4–5 in his answer: "Love the Lord your God with all your heart and with all your soul and with all your mind." Then he added, "The second is like it, 'Love your neighbor as yourself'" (Matt. 22:37–38).[10]

Since the law was first given to Moses, the command to love God has remained at the top of the list of God's requirements for humanity. We see this requirement in the last encounter between Jesus and his disciples in the book of John, when Jesus asks Peter three times, "Do you love me?" (John 21:15–17).

Here's an interesting test. First, I ask believers if they really think God loves them. Most say yes, God does. Many say so passionately. Then I ask them, "What about the reverse? Would you say you love God? If so, how do you express that love? How is that love manifested?" Many seem like they haven't given this side of the equation much thought. That worries me, because Jesus said loving God is the greatest commandment.

Throughout most of my teenage and young adult years, I came away with the impression that it was my love for Jesus that motivated me to live a faithful and fruitful life: "For Christ's love compels us . . ." (2 Cor. 5:14). It was much later in my journey that I realized that Paul's point is not that the power or motivation of *my* love matters so much, but it is *Christ's* love for *me* that gives me what I need to love my Savior. In other words, for most of my discipleship life I felt like it was up to me to try to drum up an emotion toward God. Often I was discouraged by my lack of love. But once I began to let the Bible speak and to turn this on its head—it's God's love for me that motivates me, and emotions are a reflection of receiving that—my life in Christ became more about freedom and gratitude than my emotions. This changed everything for me—as a disciple, yes, but even more importantly as a discipler of others. The outcome of this? As I let Christ's love fill me, and as I spent time thinking about it and relying on it, I found myself much more able to tap into a growing love for him inside me.

When I do cultivate my love toward Jesus, I find myself much more inclined to trust that he will help me love him. When I spend time in quiet, considering his love and beauty, focusing on my love for him, I am drawn into his embrace and my anxiety is driven away. I've come to see myself as a child whose dad is a king, who is invited to run and jump into his arms in the midst of the throne room: "Let us then approach God's throne of grace with confidence, so that we may receive mercy and find grace to help us in our time of need" (Heb. 4:16).

What would it mean for your ministry to focus on helping young people love Christ? There are many ways that followers of Christ have explored receiving God's embrace so as to increase our love for him. These fall into the category of spiritual disciplines, where we get to engage in specific activities that help us to openly receive God's love for us. There are lots of great books and articles on practicing disciplines, and busy, stressed young people often welcome user-friendly types of opportunities to come close to God. Teaching young people to love Christ is not about introducing more content but rather about providing environments and experiences that enable young people to slow down their lives and receive God's love. Instead of simply taking "prayer requests," perhaps devote most of your devotional time in gatherings to brief and easy exercises that draw students into a tangible sense of God's care and presence.

Following Christ

People in Jesus's time had an idea of what it meant to be a disciple. Back then it was common to follow a respected teacher. But in the first century "following" didn't mean following someone on social media. It meant getting up, leaving home, and actually *following* an itinerant teacher as he traveled and taught.

Many people said they wanted to follow Jesus and be his disciples, but when push came to shove they decided they had other obligations (see Luke 9:57–60). Jesus made it crystal clear. To follow him and be his disciple meant leaving everything behind. The disciples faced a decision that was both immediate and permanent.

When a man fell to his knees wanting to know how to "inherit eternal life," Jesus told him, "Go, sell everything you have and give to the poor, and you will have treasure in heaven. Then come, follow me." The man "went away sad, because he had great wealth" (Mark 10:17, 21–22).

These passages show that a true disciple can't control the timing or circumstances. You never know when Jesus will show up and ask you to follow him. All you control is the decision: Will you follow Jesus or not?

After Jesus was resurrected, he spent about forty days among his beloved followers who knew him before his death. Luke tells us that during this time he "spoke about the kingdom of God" (Acts 1:3). One of the things Jesus told his followers was, "As the Father has sent me, I am sending you" (John 20:21).

Being sent is a big part of being a disciple. That's why disciples must follow their Lord. All we in Christ are "sent ones." Being a disciple means we follow the Father's leading in Christ by the power and prompting of the Holy Spirit.

The goal of discipleship is not winning a Bible-knowledge quiz. It is living our lives in the way that Jesus did (this is why the early Christians were called "followers of the Way").[11] The goal is to become people who wholeheartedly follow Jesus and go wherever he goes.

Jesus's disciples continued to follow Christ throughout their lives. The call to follow Jesus did not end at his ascension into heaven. In a way, that was just the beginning. That's when his disciples really began to live into their calling to follow their master. And they continued, fulfilling Christ's command that they be his "witnesses . . . to the ends of the earth" (Acts 1:8).

Disciples—including you and me—must be lifelong *followers* of God, doing his work in the world, the *missio Dei*, or mission of God. This mission is to partner with the Holy Spirit in restoring all that was broken at the fall. It's a mission to usher in the kingdom of God. Every young person was created to live into their purpose. As they are invited to be contributors to God's mission in partnership with Christ and fellow believers, they are given the chance to flex their God-given muscles of being agents for God's work. This desire to be an agent of the kingdom is inbred in each one. Young people grow as disciples of Jesus when they see that they matter and have something to contribute.

What would it mean for your ministry to focus on helping young people follow Christ? As Jesus's brother James wrote, "Faith without deeds is dead" (James 2:26). To make disciples we must give young people something to *do*. Adoptive youth ministry seeks to empower kids to "do" the works of their faith—the outcome of sincere faith in Jesus that produces good for others—in a way that enhances their sense of belonging to the larger body of believers. We will look at this more deeply in chapters 9 and 10, but for now our role as disciplers is to find opportunities for kids to practice their agency for Christ in a way that contributes to the work of the whole. Student leadership may be fine for the youth ministry but rarely actually leads young people to feel like they are contributors to the body. The same goes for singing, or "teaching" four-year-olds. While these are sound expressions of using a gift in the body, to truly feel like important and valuable contributors, the young need to connect to adults while they are following Christ as he brings in his kingdom.

Trusting Christ

Most of us have heard the old chair illustration too many times, but it works. It's one thing to theoretically believe a wobbly chair is strong enough to hold you. It's a completely different thing to put that belief into action by actually trusting the chair and sitting on it.

At the beginning of this chapter we talked about *trust* in Christ being the issue. At the same time, as we unpack the fullness of how the Scriptures describe trust, it also needs to be included as a necessity for growth. Trust, then, comes fourth in our list of essentials to disciple making because, in a sense, trust is where all the preceding essentials have been leading. Trust is their fulfillment and completion. Trust means throwing ourselves into Jesus's arms, assured that he knows what's best for us.

I've used an old illustration. Now let me cite an old hymn. The one that comes to mind is the classic revival song "Trust and Obey" ("Trust and obey, for there's no other way to be happy in Jesus but to trust and obey").

In John 6:28, Jesus is being pushed by the crowds for specifics: "What must we do to do the works God requires?"

His teaching had stirred hearts, and yet people still had a hard time figuring out just what was being asked of them. Their difficulty was their background. They had been taught their whole lives that doing the laws and rituals is faith. They had an obedience-oriented faith in God. *Tell me what to do, then I will do it, and God will be satisfied.* This is the faith they were used to, where they knew the law (or at least how their leaders interpreted and enforced their understanding of the law).

Jesus spoke with a new level of authority, drawing huge crowds and capturing the attention of the multitudes. The problem was that most had no idea what to do with him. His dictates were not as simple and practical as the old system of laws. They wanted the list: do this and don't do that.

Rule following is part of what Dallas Willard calls "the gospel of sin management." As he writes in *The Divine Conspiracy*, discipleship and Christian formation can wrongly be reduced to encouraging people to perform one particular list of prescribed behaviors, and sometimes those behaviors may not reflect the teaching of Christ's gospel.[12]

Jesus made his call clear and radical: "The work of God is this: to *trust* in the one he has sent" (John 6:29, my translation).[13] The crowds wanted to pin Jesus down. He was introducing a whole new way of thinking and a new era. He had come to reshape faith. Transformation comes by *trusting in* the God of Israel, not by relying on fulfillment of the law. Christ wants us to trust him because we know him and love him, not because he demands our obedience.

It is our willingness and ability to trust God that creates the internal fertile ground for God to restore, heal, and ultimately change us into "new creations" (2 Cor. 5:17).

John tells us that even some of the disciples turned away from Christ. "From this time many of his disciples turned back and no longer followed him." Then Jesus asked his disciples, "You do not want to leave too, do you?" Simon Peter answered, "Lord, to whom shall we go? You have the words of eternal life. We have come to believe [or trust] and to know that you are the Holy One of God" (John 6:66–68).

Jesus made clear what his mission was: he, God incarnate, had come "to seek and to save the lost" (Luke 19:10). Therefore, the "work" of those who would follow him was not to "do" but to receive his love, mercy, and power, and obey him by trusting in him. This has not changed, for the same conversation is at the heart of discipleship today. In whom do I place my trust?

How can your ministry focus on helping young people trust Christ? By showing them that our faith is less about behavior and more about trust. When they want to know about drinking alcohol, for example, our response is not really about drinking but rather about what it means to trust Christ in the midst of the social pressure of consuming alcohol. My response to the issue of underage drinking, or any other behavior, reflects my willingness and ability to trust Christ. This should form the way that we think, teach, and lead in regard to ethics and behavior. To know, love, and follow Jesus Christ ultimately comes down to one question: Will I trust him with my life?

Discipleship in an Adoptive Church

As God's chosen agents we have been commissioned to "make disciples" who know, love, follow, trust, and therefore obey Jesus Christ. This is our ministry to young people. To do our part in the making of Christ followers, we must ensure that everything we say, program, plan, and do reflects this ultimate calling.

Because we are called to make disciples in Jesus's name, and we know that disciples have a far greater opportunity to trust and follow Christ in a welcoming, nurturing, and empowering community, adoptive churches seek to create an environment where each disciple walks alongside other disciples of Jesus.

Again, we're back to the soil analogy. If you want plants to thrive in God's big family garden, focus on nurturing the environment where such plants can flourish.

5

The Goal of Ministry in an Adoptive Church

Two responses to adoptive youth ministry keep ringing in my head. Both were from smart and experienced youth ministry leaders, one of whom was especially likely to give me a pass simply because I was impassioned when I talked about it. But, frankly, neither was sold.

The first said, "I don't see why I need adoptive youth ministry. I already do that. Chap, what's the big deal?"

And the second said, "What you're describing is already true. We don't have to actually *do* anything. God has adopted us, and so the Bible sometimes describes us in family terms. But Jesus never talked this way, and Paul uses the language sparingly, and never in a ministry context. So what's the big deal?"

The responses were the same: "What's the big deal?"

I love youth ministry. I love youth ministry thinking and thinkers. I love kids. And I love the frenzied diversity of the church, warts and all. At the same time, I wish that the way we have been and are doing youth ministry was the complete picture of what God is asking of us. As good as our progress has been, I can't escape the feeling that we've still got to take one more step, one more leap, to do all we can to give our young the best shot at deep and lasting faith. For me that step is forming an adoptive church. Let me explain.

Keeping Your Eye on the End

So far we have explored the idea of adoptive ministry and connected that to making disciples of young people. We have looked at the essentials of adoptive ministry. Now it's time to start thinking about putting it into practice.

As we head into implementation, the critical beginning point is to be crystal clear on where we want to end up. To do anything well, we need to know the destination. In the case of ministry, to create a structure and strategy we need to know the outcomes we're going for. Yes, we know we want young people to know and follow Christ. But what would that mean and look like for a young college student or a twenty-seven-year-old teacher?

So let's define the goal of adoptive youth ministry. These are my words; they may not be yours. The way I use words and the way you or your team uses words will be different. This description is intended to help you understand the essential elements of adoptive youth ministry.

The Goal of Adoptive Youth Ministry

To create an environment where young people are encouraged to live into their calling in Christ as agents of the kingdom within the household of God.

While we have already addressed some basic elements of this statement, let's explore each of the three key phrases as we prepare to implement adoptive ministry.

To Create an Environment Where Young People Are Encouraged . . .

Our most basic task in adoptive youth ministry is the environment we create for kids. Our content, our creativity, our innovation, even the numbers or quality of paid staff and leaders we have to run a great program will make very little impact if kids do not feel like they are safe, warm, and welcome.

It doesn't take tenured scholars to figure out that people run from a *cold* social environment and flock to a *warm* one (although many have actually studied and repeatedly shown this to be true).

Think about your church. Would you describe it, if you had to make a choice, as a warm or a cold environment? This means everything from the parking to the signage to the way that people are greeted as they arrive. What about the worship service? How about church potlucks and socials, or mission trips and camps? Is your church, in sum, a generally warm church or a cold church? This is important because young people don't like a cold environment.[1] Who does?

Now carry this into your youth ministry (or *any* ministry, as the same sociological principle applies). If you can, imagine walking into your large group gathering, or a small group, or heading to camp. Would you say that these are warm or cold? You might, for example, feel like the way you do small groups is warm (in homes, with safe conversations, everyone seems genuinely comfortable). Yet when you're honest, you may say that your room is set to the liking of the leaders rather than a warm environment for the students. A warm environment is crucial to even begin to create an adoptive ministry mindset and program. Otherwise, even for those who do continue to show up, they will have a hard time dropping their guard and truly trusting the adults.

In addition to being warm, does what you do—including everything from what happens in the parking lot to how kids or emerging adults are greeted when they enter a room to the aesthetics (music, lighting, room setup)—reflect the intention to make sure young people know that they are welcomed members of the community? This isn't about spending money, but about commitment and intention. With even what we may consider the little things—like announcements or slides or teaching—everything we create, say, and do comes into play to create a warm or cold ministry environment. In an adoptive ministry mindset, our goal is to make sure that everything young people experience screams out at them: "This is *your* place. This is *your* church. This is *your* family!"

Last, and most important, do the people—everyone who represents the ministry or the church—convey a warmth toward every single young person, wherever and whoever they are? Are adults well trained to know that the goal of ministry to the young is to create a welcoming environment and everything else flows from there? Every young person deserves and longs for three things when they enter a room:

- to know they've been seen (so we look them in the eye)
- to hear their name
- to have a genuine encounter with someone who says something nice to them

These are very simple things: eye contact, name recognition, and hearing something nice that connects with them. *But many kids go to church and even youth groups and rarely if ever receive that kind of personal touch.* Adoptive youth ministry creates connection. Because of the relational environment we are called to create, adults must be trained to know that the meeting starts when the first student shows up and it is not over until the last kid leaves. Our focus on environment, especially the relational environment, is so crucial that it should be the source from which all other ministry flows.

. . . to Live into Their Calling in Christ as Agents of the Kingdom . . .

The biblical and theological content of adoptive youth ministry, as we saw in chapter 4, is not as concerned with behavior or even raw cognitive knowledge (though certainly those things matter as aspects of our discipleship) as with helping students to see and hear Jesus for themselves as they engage him in community. Historically, so much of Christian discipleship has been reduced to *doing* Christianity instead of *living into* a trust in Christ that is so central and powerful that it becomes our vocation for life. Our vocation is not what is on our business card or where we receive our paycheck. It is our calling as Christ's followers. Jesus was clear about this: "Whoever wants to be my disciple must deny themselves and take up their cross daily and follow me" (Luke 9:23). Our role in adoptive youth ministry, then, is to help our young people come to see Jesus Christ and the gospel as the calling that God has for them.

As this whole book will reinforce, the central image for adoptive ministry is the gift of the incarnation mentioned in John 1:12—"the right to become children of God"—and this means that in the household of God the young are siblings of the old. Although few people actually talk this way about the nature of who we are together in the body of Christ, biblically there are no exceptions to this truth. Because this biblical concept is rarely talked about, perhaps this idea might at first be difficult to imagine. This will be among the most challenging hurdles you will face as you work to convince your church that it is the explicit responsibility of adults in the church to view and treat young people as their little brothers and sisters. This language alone, as people begin to get on board, can move a congregation from being slightly cold to increasingly warm. However you describe this, recognition of the co-sibling nature of the church is a necessity for adoptive youth ministry to make a dent in how young people feel about your church, or even about the Christian faith in general. If they don't feel respected, included, and welcomed, why would they bother to remain?

As we encourage the young to live into their calling, a key word pops out of the stated goal: "*agents* of the kingdom." We will look more carefully at the idea of agency in future chapters, but for now we have to at least make sure we understand its importance. Theologically, we do not bring in the kingdom or even change the world. Our mission, to be biblical, must always be God's mission. We are given the privilege of walking alongside God and following the promptings of the Holy Spirit as we grow to understand what God has in store for us and calls us to. This is the definition of agency: I am given power and purpose to contribute to God's missional work. There are few adults and fewer adult-run systems and institutions that train the young in the exercise of their God-given agency. From the time they are little, youth are taught to do as they're told and speak when spoken to. But God has bigger things in store for his children, and for his church. Yes, this is a church issue as much as a youth ministry issue, but in adoptive youth ministry the outcome of faithful biblical discipleship is unleashing the power of the Holy Spirit in God's called agents.

. . . within the Household of God

This phrase is what sets adoptive ministry apart from other ways of envisioning youth ministry. If it lacked "within the household of God," the goal could be seen as what every youth ministry does, or at least strives to do. In youth ministry circles, we have talked for years about energizing lifelong faith and the goal of nurturing passionate young people who are set free to follow hard after God. We have also worked to create an environment where kids feel safe and heard and loved, both within the youth group and by broader church leadership. In 1989, Wayne Rice's *Up Close and Personal: How to Build Community in Your Youth Group* reflected what was becoming a new focus in youth ministry practice.[2] Rice's thinking, which still pervades youth ministry today, is that being a follower of Christ is not a solitary journey but a communal one. This was a major step forward for understanding a theology of discipleship. Community matters.

Since then, leaders in youth ministry have recognized that we must move beyond simply building community: we need to strengthen the connections outside the adolescent peer group. This became the next wave of focus for youth ministry, and we now express this in two fundamental arenas: parent ministry and intergenerational ministry. In most churches, parent ministry has become an aspect of student ministry, at least in partnership with what has come to be called "family ministry." And more recently the push for intergenerational ministry has become part of the overall youth ministry strategy. Both of these trends, like Rice's book, represented further steps toward a more holistic and long-term view of ministry to the young. In churches where parent and child relationships are being encouraged and strengthened and where older generations are more connected to emerging generations, the youth ministry itself has become healthier, and deeper faith among the young is often a result.

To many, these emphases—proactively connecting teenagers and emerging adults to one another, to their families, and to adults in a congregation—have basically settled the issue of what it means for youth ministry "to create an environment where young people are able to live into their calling in Christ as agents of the kingdom." Why bother, then, with adoptive ministry? What is the difference?

Let's start with peer community. As helpful as intergroup relationships are to giving teenagers a sense of community, teenagers need more than what peers have to offer them. Young people have been raised in a culture of rampant isolation that has been described as *atomized*, defined as "to treat as made up of many discrete units."[3] There are many aspects to and reasons for this, but perhaps the most significant is the dissolution of social support for the young from adults and adult-controlled settings and systems, causing them to grow up feeling like they must live for the agenda of others and find a sense of place by "playing to the crowd."[4] Thus, to survive as a child, teenager, and emerging adult, young people are taught that they must perform their way into blessing. As a result, emerging generations are desperate for support, for nurture, for guidance, and for hope. As the old adage goes, two kids in a mud puddle can't clean each other up. Someone needs to come to them with a helping hand and a clean towel.

But aren't intergenerational ministry and multigenerational relationships the antidote to the systemic abandonment of the young? If we just encourage the old and the young to walk together, to care for each other, isn't that enough for young people to feel connected to the body of Christ?

Yes and no.

Yes, it is better than what youth ministry has been doing. Any meaningful connections are important and helpful to the overall health and psyche of an adolescent and emerging adult.

But relational connectedness *on its own* is not enough to convince a young person that they are welcome and that they are vital members of a community. Sometimes, just by the nature of how a church or even a handful of adults live out their commitment to the young intergenerationally, they end up functionally applying adoptive ministry. But intentionally encouraging cross-generational relationships, or even programmatically strengthening mentoring relationships across a wide age demographic, does not necessarily offer an important piece of what young people need: contributing purpose.

This is why the goal of adoptive youth ministry has as its trajectory "*within* the household of God." A biblically driven youth ministry not only nurtures but also empowers the young to participate and contribute to the life of the body. The Scriptures make clear that everyone in the body of Christ is essential to the vitality of the community (see 1 Cor. 12 as one example). The aim of adoptive youth ministry, then, is to ensure that every person experiences life in a diverse family where everyone they meet treats them with the respect of a beloved younger sibling.

Why does this matter? The answer lies in the goal of adoptive youth ministry: that every adult would provide for every young person a hand and a towel, to lift them up and help wash the mud from their eyes.

PART TWO

The Structure of an Adoptive Church

We've explored the theology and goals of adoptive ministry. Now let's see how we can build a ministry structure that produces the kind of environment where young people can experience what it means to be adopted among fellow God-ordained siblings.

I wish I could give you an easy-to-follow model, but adoptive ministry is a way of thinking more than a model. This section will help you create your own expression of adoptive youth ministry in your context, beginning with a chapter on creating a contextually applied structure for the goal of your ministry.

But you can't do everything alone. Chapters 7 and 8 are about getting the right people "on the bus"[1] to join you in making adoptive youth ministry a reality. The more fellow adoptees you bring into the fold of adoptive ministry, the more likely kids and young adults will be able to connect with your community.

6

Implementing Adoptive
Youth Ministry

'm sold," the youth and family pastor of a large church in Canada told me. "So . . . *how*?"

As I have thought and prayed, studied and written about the idea of adoptive ministry, everywhere I go I try to get people on board. I'm not proposing something that is not already there right in front of us. Throughout the Scriptures the idea of God's children being part of a family is prominent. When I talk about our goal in youth ministry, adoptive youth ministry fits, conceptually at least, for almost everybody. Whether in an hour seminar at a convention or an all-day denominational gathering, seeing the church as a family and proactively helping kids to make it a family is not a hard intellectual leap. So, inevitably, what everybody wants to know is, "How do I pull it off?"

Pulling It Off

In part 1 we focused on the heartbeat and driving goal of adoptive youth ministry:

To create an environment where young people are encouraged to live into their calling in Christ as agents of the kingdom within the household of God.

To put adoptive youth ministry into practice means that everything we do moves us toward that goal. When it comes to putting on the wheels that lead to that, or any, goal—structure, overall strategy, programs, staffing, calendar, and so on—we need to take several steps. Here is what it takes to develop and implement a ministry that reaches the ministry goal or desired outcomes. It's called *developing a contextually applied structure.*

Developing a Contextually Applied Structure

1. *Establishing a clear goal:* committing to going after the goal together
2. *Analyzing context:* knowing who you are and where you've been
3. *Assessing and identifying resources:* knowing your ministry options
4. *Tweaking (or creating) structure:* putting a plan into place
5. *Gathering your partners:* finding and equipping those who matter
6. *Equipping the team:* getting partners in the right spot

This chapter will explore strategies 1–4, and the following two chapters will go deeply into strategies 5 and 6.

Establishing a Clear Goal: Committing to Going after the Goal Together

Organizational theorists Carl Larson and Frank LaFasto spent lots of time working to understand teams. They looked at successful teams and unsuccessful teams. They interviewed cohesive teams and observed fragmented and even contentious teams. What they found is that people who are effective in collectively going after a goal almost always have a set of common characteristics. The most significant marker relates to how clear the end goal is to every team member. When everyone can describe their group's goal precisely, if not with the exact same wording, they are far more likely to reach their goal than a group that does not share that feature.[1] Regardless of the setting—from professional sports to business to NASA—this prominent characteristic was universally consistent.

In ministry settings, all too often the goals we have are too generic to meaningfully connect with people as they do their part toward the goal, or ministries do not have a clear goal in the first place. With adoptive youth ministry, however, the goal is always front and center. The trick for us, then, is to make people aware of both its meaning and the implications of its pursuit. This means that a seventh-grade small group leader should know, understand, and be able to articulate the goal of the youth ministry in the same way as the people who flip the burgers for the monthly family ministry gathering of students and adults.

To make sure that everyone who affects the work of adoptive youth ministry understands the goal (and it's a very small list of people in a church who do not!), it is up to leadership, however you define that, to make it happen. The two key words for this are *communication* and *training*. Communication can be defined as "the art of being understood."[2] To be strategic communicators of adoptive youth ministry, we must get the word out far and wide, with a consistent and clear message. This includes everything from casual conversations to training materials, from announcements and sermons during services to how we introduce parents to the vision. We need to think macro, bringing along the whole church, and micro, leading individuals who are on the front lines—like parents, church and lay leadership, and youth ministry staff and volunteers—to know what it means for them to move toward adoptive ministry. We must make sure not only that people know what the long-term vision is but also that they see their role in it.

Related to communication is training. We must train a congregation, including the distant pew sitters as well as those in positions of leadership, so that people know what adoptive ministry means not only for the youth ministry but for them as well. Parents, for example, should be trained and equipped to partner with the church in helping their children enter into deeper relationships within a congregation (with appropriate boundaries for safety). Older congregants should be deliberately equipped to serve the young as older siblings who have the ability to both nurture and empower, and give voice to them when the opportunity arises. Those who preach need to be brought up to speed on their role in sharing content, telling stories, and describing what it means to be part of the household of God.

These and many other subsets of the community need to hear how they play a crucial role in creating the environment where adoptive ministry can flourish, as well as providing the presence and commitment to nurturing and empowering the young as they grow. And most of all, everyone should engage the Scriptures to explore what it means when Jesus calls the "least of these" his "brothers and sisters" (Matt. 25:40) and the implications of his command to "love each other" (John 15:17).

Analyzing Context: Knowing Who You Are and Where You've Been

I was recently asked by an older pastor from a relatively small church, "Who is doing this?"

"Lots of churches, mostly in bits and pieces, and usually by accident," I answered.

"It would be great if you could give us a *model* so we can see adoptive ministry in action. You know, how it works in context."

First, let's look at the positives of this feedback. Yes, I do see many if not most churches offering some sort of adoptive ministry in what they do. I know of a few that intentionally claim to be a "youth-friendly" or "family-friendly" church, and they work hard to be as intergenerationally welcoming as they can. Another church I know works hard at welcoming the young when they have the opportunity. When they invite teenagers to serve in their music ministry, for example, they make sure all the adults know that the student is not simply another musician or singer—a helpful tool—but a young person who "deserves our care [nurture] and encouragement [in this case almost a pseudonym for empowerment]." These examples—and I've encountered many—are, to be sure, signs of an adoptive style of ministry. In this sense there are lots of snapshots out there of churches wanting to draw the young into their community.[3]

But, if pressed, I would hesitate to call these faith communities *models* of adoptive youth ministry. When we look at the positives scattered throughout the ecclesial landscape, even those churches that seek to be youth- or family-friendly or that sporadically bring an adolescent into an otherwise adult role are rarely proactive in becoming a family of siblings, which is the basic theological premise of adoptive ministry. It is heartening to see the recent trend of many people and churches sincerely working to reach out to the young. Encouraging young people to use their gifts for ministry and enlisting adults who care about teenagers enough to walk alongside them does provide the conceptual seedbed for adoptive youth ministry. After all, the hardest part of adoptive ministry is getting people over the hump of thinking this means adopting kids (which, as I've repeatedly said, it does not). So as of now there are churches that have been intrigued by the idea of adoptive ministry (whether they name it that or not), where a community is committed to living into their mutual adoption in Christ and treating one another, regardless of age or status, as siblings (whether they use that language or not). But are there particular models to point to as prototypes to emulate and copy? To me this is a harder question. Not because people are not going after the basic premises of adoptive ministry, but because the notion of models can be a slippery thing.

This reveals an even more important issue, and hopefully a comforting one, when it comes to implementing a vision for any form of ministry, and especially something as organic as adoptive ministry. The "fly in the ointment"[4] of models is that your church is unique, and so is everyone else's! Here is just a sampling of the ways your setting is unique:

- history: why you are where you are
- narratives: how you describe your church, even to yourself
- theological assumptions: beyond faith statement or denomination, the particulars that your church tends to camp out on
- cultural assumptions: how your community sees the world, both in the big picture and around you

Once we have communicated and fostered a conversation that helps people think of their faith in terms of their mutual adoption in Christ, the next step is to expand that into what it means to them as a community. Then, in light of this theological reality, we can begin to examine how we've seen ourselves in relation to one another in the past, not just in student ministry but across the community. How have we operated as a community of siblings in the household of God? Have outsiders, or those in various ministry groups (seniors, college students, young adults, middle schoolers, singles), felt connected to the rest of the congregation in a manner anywhere close to something that could be described as siblings in Christ? These are bedrock questions for any church to ask of itself: Who have we been, and who do we think we are . . . together?

This is what it means to objectively and honestly examine our context. To move toward an adoptive community of intimately and interconnected siblings—the kind that Jesus exhibits with his disciples and followers throughout his ministry, and Paul and the other New Testament writers implicitly and even explicitly remind us about on almost every page—we need to be clear about where we have been, where we are now, and why we are who we are. This is our context.

Take your history, for example. If you are a twenty-five-year-old church that was started in the heyday of the "seeker" movement, then likely that will tell you not only where you've been but also where you are currently headed. In the early years the seeker movement, to many at least, was about church growth, bringing in either people who were overtly described as "unchurched" or those lukewarm regarding faith. The hurdle for you might have been, and probably currently is, taking people deeper in their faith than an initial, "Hey, I like this. This is church? I'm in!" Your congregation, then, might not even realize how the Scriptures call us through faith into a new family. This history will affect not how adoptive youth ministry needs to be communicated but how it will need to be strategically implemented.

Let's take this same example further. Your congregation, and maybe even some staff, may not have a very rich understanding of what it means to be adopted into God's family. So a careful read on that history and resultant current setting might instruct you to be more deliberate in guiding the community to a place of recognizing what it actually means to live "in Christ" together.[5] To be given the right to become children of God by receiving and believing in Jesus Christ (John 1:12) implicitly means that before we believe and receive Christ, we are orphaned, at least as far as our relationship to God is concerned. Once we come to faith, then, we not only have the right (or privilege) to become children of God with other children, but we have an explicit responsibility to live according to that truth. In many congregations this is news to people. That, then, is a contextual issue that is part and parcel of the implementation of an adoptive youth ministry.

Context, as I've said, is anything and everything you can think of that would affect your ability to establish a welcoming community that sees itself, by God's grace and declaration, as a family of siblings. Knowing where you have been and who you are, in every way you can imagine, provides the data that will help you define what is likely to be confusing or missed in your community and emphasize what needs to be strengthened.

Assessing and Identifying Resources: Knowing Your Ministry Options

Implementing a strategy committed to adoptive youth ministry begins with knowing where you've been, where you are, and where you believe that you are headed. That is the context. The next step is to assess and identify the resources you have available to enter into that context with adoptive youth ministry as the driving goal.

Resources can be defined as anything that affects your ability to achieve your goal, although the term is rarely used this way. What this means is that resources can be either positive or negative, depending on how you understand and make use of them. Resources are, in fact, neutral. They are neither good nor bad. This understanding is important because we tend to consider resources as what we have and what we don't have but think we need, or at least want. This is where we get into trouble in ministry, because it is easy for us to be held back from freely engaging our call as a result of what we perceive is a lack of the resources we need to do our jobs. "We could really make an impact, but we don't have enough male leaders to do what we want to do." In this example, while you might have identified what you envision doing to move forward, currently the staff you have makes that untenable. So, yes, "pray to the Lord of the harvest" for people to serve alongside you (Matt. 9:36–38), but don't let your perception of these kinds of deficits hold you back. Instead, find creative ways to adjust your plans and even your expectations to match your resources. Our job is to do what we can with what God has given us, and to pray for whatever else the Lord may want to give us to enable us to follow the vision he has for us.

The following list provides examples of resources that affect your ability—positively or negatively—to create the environment and offer the content and strategy for an adoptive youth ministry:

- the paid staff and volunteers you have currently (including but not limited to their age, gender, personal and spiritual maturity, time availability, etc.)

- your programmatic history and current momentum (beware of tossing programs that have momentum, and be honest about those that do not)
- facilities (don't limit this to the church building(s), but think outside the box; what are some other options right in front of you that you hadn't considered before, like a park, a community center, homes, a school)
- the way you have structured your ministry—how you serve middle school, high school, post–high school, and emerging adults in your community (whatever structure you have had is simply the way you have divided people, so allow this history to inform what has been good and not so good, especially as it pertains to the implementation of an adoptive ministry)
- attitudes of parents, staff, and other adults in the congregation

In ministry, it is important to remember that whatever God has given us is sufficient to do and be what God is asking of us. We can and should pray for the resources we think we need to serve him well. But all the while, the Lord only asks of us to be faithful with what he has given us.

Tweaking (or Creating) Structure: Putting a Plan into Place

One of the hallmarks of adoptive youth ministry is that it does not rely on programs but sees them as useful tools. *What* we do is far less important than *how* we go about creating an environment where young people believe that they matter and are welcome in the larger body. After a thorough assessment of both your context and resources, you might find that you will only need to make minor adjustments to your programs and structure. In this case, you might find you have to put most of your energies into convincing and training your team and the congregation. Or perhaps you realize that you have historically put so much emphasis on separating your high school students from congregants and the church at large that you now need to think differently and maybe even implement changes. It may take some careful work and time, but you might decide to loosen your grip on having a strict high school ministry identity and to relationally diffuse discipleship strategies, especially for eleventh- and twelfth-grade students, across the broader church (handing off students to the missions committee or a pastoral care team, for example). The point is not to change things for change's sake but to be realistic and strategic as you move in the direction of adoptive ministry.

As you begin to put a plan into place, there are two vital components to keep in mind: building consensus and committing to regular evaluations. Building consensus is more than informing or even training people. It is including people in gathering data as you analyze your context and resources. It is inviting others to examine and give input on what you have found and concluded. And perhaps most important, it is moving slowly with great care, especially if you will begin tinkering with established programs, events, retreats, or anything else in which someone may feel like you are taking something they cherish from them. As Harvard's Ronald Heifitz has said, "What people resist is not change per se, but loss."[6] Any time you are going to do anything different from what people appreciate or expect, even if they are vocal naysayers about it, the more they are given the opportunity to own the process of change, the greater your chances of systemic success.

Evaluating Your Ministry

Finally, as you begin to build a revised or even wholly new ministry to become an adoptive ministry, right from the start you should develop a written, broadly communicated, and clear evaluation plan. This evaluation should not be on how a program is doing on its own merit (as in, "Youth group seems to be going well—our numbers are up, our kids are engaged, and parents are pleased") but rather on how well it is moving toward the goal of adoptive ministry. Programmatic pieces and individual events may be powerful, growing, and hugely popular on their own, but if they do not lead toward the goal of adoptive youth ministry, then for most students their lasting impact will likely be slim at best.

The way to create an evaluative tool is to start with your goal. For our purposes let's use my goal of adoptive youth ministry:

> To create an environment where young people are encouraged to live into their calling in Christ as agents of the kingdom within the household of God.

Next, break the goal into its key component parts (as we did in chapter 5) and create a series of statements that connect the program or event to your goal. For each of these questions, provide a Likert scale (1–5) and a space for comments.

Using my goal as an example to evaluate, for instance, a high school small group ministry, here's what an evaluation sheet could look like:

Student Ministries Program Evaluation

Name of evaluator: _____

Date: _____

Our Vision
Youth Ministries at First Church is committed to creating an environment where young people are encouraged to live into their calling in Christ as agents of the kingdom within the household of God.

Evaluation of High School Small Groups
On a scale of 1 to 5, circle what best describes your view and please comment:

1. The program **creates an environment** where young people live into their calling.

Yes, directly	Yes, but indirectly	Possibly, but incrementally	By accident	Not at all
1	2	3	4	5

Comments:_____

_____

_____

2. The program encourages young people to **live into their calling** in Christ as agents of the kingdom.

Yes, directly	Yes, but indirectly	Possibly, but incrementally	By accident	Not at all
1	2	3	4	5

Comments:_____

_____

_____

3. The program encourages young people to be **participants and contributors alongside their siblings in Christ** within the household of God.

Yes, directly	Yes, but indirectly	Possibly, but incrementally	By accident	Not at all
1	2	3	4	5

Comments:_____

_____

_____

An evaluation tool should be created for every ministry program or event. Distribute it as widely as possible (such as students, parents, volunteers, pastoral staff, and so on) both to build a sense of ownership in your community and to discover any issues or patterns that a single leader or a small handful of people might miss. Evaluations like this should be done frequently, and each program or event will dictate its own timetable. Of course, leadership must take seriously what is revealed in the evaluation process and adjust the ministry plan accordingly.

Implementing adoptive youth ministry in your setting begins with making sure everyone understands and buys into the goal of what it is you are trying to accomplish not only in youth ministry but for the entire faith community. Once you have begun this work, assessing your context, identifying your resources, and building your structure will enable you to strategically move young people into greater inclusion and empowerment in your church. All that's left is to gather your partners and train your team for the move to adoptive ministry. The fun has just begun.

7

The Power of Partners

Rich was the kind of youth worker whom people—young and old—loved to love. He was in his midtwenties, warm, fun to be with (if occasionally flippant), and self-confident. But on the day when I sat down with Rich for lunch, he was frustrated. A week earlier, one of the church parents had complained to the pastor about Rich's work.

"Don't they realize they have one of the best youth workers in the city?" asked Rich, who had been on the job about eight months, and whose youth ministry training consisted of two seminary classes, a few conferences, and long hours spent googling teaching exercises.

Rich was just getting started, his anger adding heat to his words.

"It's not just parents griping," he said. "Senior leaders in this church don't get youth ministry. Even other people on the staff don't get it. None of them really care about kids!"

Then he looked me in the eye and revealed the thing that was really getting under his skin.

"You know, Chap, the worst thing is that these people don't realize I am the youth expert in the church."

Unfortunately, Rich is not the only one who feels this way!

When I consulted with one congregation, my first Sunday at the church coincided with that all-too-common annual event known as "Youth Sunday." The student band was enthusiastic, if not stellar. Kids successfully led the announcements, prayer, and Scripture readings. The congregation seemed to be engaged.

But when it came time for the sermon, the mood shifted. That's because one of the church youth workers got up and began his sermon with this bombshell: "This is Youth Sunday, my favorite Sunday of the year," he said. "Do you know why? Because it is the one day a year the youth pastor can yell at the parents!"

Partnership in Youth Ministry

These comments may sound unusual, yet in my experience they are anything but outliers. They represent the attitudes of so many youth workers I have known: a Lone Ranger spirit that seems to reside deep in the psyche of youth ministry leaders.

Partly that's because many of the men and women who decide to take on the role of youth pastor in the first place are drawn in by the independent, high-energy, fast-paced entrepreneurial nature of the job. Such freedom helps them deal with the less exciting parts of the job: the low pay, the low status in the church pecking order, and the "fishbowl" lifestyle expectations that come along with serving young people and adults.

I've seen it too many times. Enthusiastic leaders arrive on the scene raring to go, but in time their lack of experience, the low income, and the constant criticism from adults wear them down, with some of them becoming relational train wrecks.

In many ways it's understandable why so many youth ministry workers feel like they have to "fight" their churches (including the parents, staff, and leadership) to do their job. That's why youth work can end up being a life-draining and isolated job.

But people like Rich often have deeper problems to consider. Their ministry models have led them to believe that they alone are called and equipped to minister to young people. They seek control and authority instead of teamwork and cooperation. They want to be CEOs, not servants.

In the rest of this chapter I want to point to a better way.

Two Ways to Lead

There are two kinds of leaders, whether you are leading a youth group or a Fortune 500 corporation.

The *"I'm in charge" leadership model* gives those in charge the ultimate control, putting them atop the personnel flowchart. Dominant leaders often sound like Rich, defending their turf and chasing off others who seek to influence their work.

The *partnering leadership model* sees ministry in a completely different sense. Here, the youth worker is the first among equals in the community of faith, not a dictatorial head of a hierarchy.

Let's unpack these two models.

The "I'm in Charge" Leadership Model

"I'm in charge" leaders believe it's their job to "do" the ministry. Others may be involved and may even be valuable players in the ministry. But from the perspective of the leader, other people are there to serve the ministry that the leader is responsible for. Those who "help" may feel a sense of purpose and even ownership, yet in the end they come and go, and ultimately their job is to support the person in charge.

The other people who work within this model do not feel valued; they feel used. They wonder if they are contributing in a meaningful way, since the leader seems to be the source of all the action. Serving under a dominating leader can be tough. People rarely feel deep loyalty to such leaders, and this leads to a revolving door of volunteers who need to be regularly replenished.

Meanwhile, parents, congregational leaders (lay and staff), and others not directly involved in the ministry are seen as outsiders who are appreciated when they are supportive and criticized or even shunned when they are not. With this style of leadership, the leader receives praise when things go well (which is certainly one of the major motivators for this style), but they also can feel ignored (or worse) when things go sideways.

In some cases, this approach can breed a "hero cult" that gives leaders all of the power and authority. They are in charge, and they are responsible for bringing transformation to the people they serve. If you listen carefully, you can hear dominant leaders referring to their work as "my ministry" and to those who help as "my volunteers."

When this dominant approach goes well, everyone is pleased and grateful. When it falls apart, the leader becomes lonely, isolated, defensive, and discouraged. That's when people reach their limit: "Fire him, and bring on the next one!"

The Partnering Leadership Model

The other leadership style, which is far less common in practice, starts from a completely different conception. Instead of the dominating approach of "I'm the boss, and we will do it my way," the partnering leader says, "Thanks for joining us in this great and glorious effort. We're all in this together!"

The partnering approach is based on the concept of first among equals (*primus inter pares*, in Latin). That's why some leaders refer to this model as "primus leadership."

Here's how management consultant Sarah Alexander describes the difference: "The 'Primus Inter Pares' approach to leadership—first among equals—offers us a new way of managing and leading in the 21st century. With this approach all employees are seen as equals, regardless of their position or status."[1]

The theology supporting the partnering leadership approach echoes Paul's reminders to the church at Corinth that they are all equal members of God's household: "Those parts of the body that seem to be weaker are indispensable, and the parts that we think are less honorable we treat with special honor. And the parts that are unpresentable are treated with special modesty, while our presentable parts need no special treatment. But God has put the body together, giving greater honor to the parts that lacked it, so that there should be no division in the body, but that its parts should have equal concern for each other" (1 Cor. 12:22–25).

In the partnering leadership model, every person is valued. Every person is recognized as gifted. Every person is celebrated as important. Every person knows that they are a vital element of the ministry—even if they flip burgers or drive a van, each one matters.

The leader's role is to lead—not dominate—and the community affirms that role and recognizes the leader's unique gifts. But the partnering leader also affirms the roles and gifts of others. The role of the leader is to ensure that everyone's voice is heard, everyone's contribution is celebrated, and everyone has a sense of ownership.

Comparing the Models

These two very different ways of leading come from opposite perspectives on who owns the ministry.

The top-down, controlling management style, the "I'm in charge" leadership model, is predicated on the idea that the person hired as youth leader is the one person who is the most knowledgeable, the most vital, and the most capable of making the mission successful.

The partnering leadership model is based on a collegial community of equally capable people, each bringing their own unique gifts and talents, and each committed to the group's mission.

In my experience, the top-down model is the norm in most churches and youth groups, while the partnering model is the more biblical— and ultimately more effective—of the two models. It should be clear from the previous chapters that I believe the adoptive youth ministry approach requires the partnering model of leadership to thrive.

When a congregation operates out of a leader-driven (and often staff-driven) orientation to ministry, people typically fall in line with that model. Adoptive ministry, on the other hand, requires a *participatory* community where the people—God's gathered siblings—invite, welcome, nurture, and empower adolescents and emerging adults to join them in the life and mission of the community.

A leader-centered, "I'm in charge" church faces challenges drawing in young people because the life and mission of the church are less about participation than about observation and conformity. These are precisely the characteristics that drive the young away from the organized church. Only an adoptive community can receive the young and offer an adoptive youth ministry.

This chart contrasts the ways the two leadership styles play out in ministry:

A Partnering Leader versus an "I'm in Charge" Leader

A Partnering Leader	An "I'm in Charge" Leader
Encourages others' attempts	Sabotages others' efforts
Points out others' strong points	Brings attention to others' faults
Sees flaws as opportunities for growth	Uses others' flaws as ammunition
Readily admits own mistakes	Is defensive and justifies mistakes
Gives away credit to others	Demands or manipulates credit
Rejoices when others succeed	Is jealous of others' successes
Is excited when others do it better	Is easily intimidated
Is willing to risk to improve	Plays it safe to retain position
Is content to remain in the background	Requires others to notice
Is a builder of teams	Defaults to doing things himself or herself

Adapted from Wayne Cordeiro, *Doing Church as a Team* (Ventura, CA: Regal, 2001), 112, and found in Bill MacPhee, "Adoptive Leadership," in *Adoptive Youth Ministry*, ed. Chap Clark (Grand Rapids: Baker Academic, 2016), 282–83.

Depending on your particular church or ministry environment, the "I'm in change" model may seem to work pretty well, at least in the short run, particularly if the leader is blessed with a good teaching style and various charismatic gifts. Over time, however, the wheels come off because there's no one person who possesses everything a ministry needs to function well. Not Rich. Not you. Not me.

But that doesn't stop certain youth leaders from trying to prove that they are God's chosen superstars. And unfortunately, this top-down approach can actually hinder students' willingness to let down their guard and invite other adults into their lives and their personal stories.

For adoptive youth ministry to make a lasting impact in an increasingly atomized culture, we need to build bridges of trust and care with students who are desperate to engage and learn from a wide array of adults. This kind of inclusive team approach empowers young people as they venture into the new waters of congregational inclusion.

The Journey from Dominating to Partnering

As you've read about Rich and the two ministry leadership approaches, does it seem like you're a dominating rather than a partnering leader? If so, what can you do to change your organizational culture and transition to the partnering model?

Often the motive to be a controlling leader springs more from largely unexamined assumptions about how leadership works rather than from serious theological study or perspective.

As representatives of Jesus Christ and the kingdom of God, our main concern is not so much to be "good leaders" as to be faithful stewards of the mission we are called to serve. Each of us has our own unique blind spots, our own unique temptations to amass power and lord it over others.

In some cases, churches and Christian youth organizations worsen these temptations. A job description, church leadership, or even members of the congregation may even demand a strong leader. They want somebody to take charge, be in control, and make others follow.

But there are significant philosophical conflicts between this approach and the adoptive youth ministry model. In the long run, the partnering model works best to create an inclusive collegial community of invested adults working together for the greater goal of helping young people live into their mutual adoption in Christ.

The transition from a dominating model to a partnering model happens best not through theological debate but through looking at how one lives, reflecting on Christ's ministry, welcoming the Holy Spirit's influence, and embracing the opportunity to serve alongside others rather than dominating them.

Here are four ways any organization or community can move from an "I'm in charge" style of leadership to a more partnering, adoptive approach:

1. Teach how the Bible describes the unity and diversity of gifts in the body, and how leadership's job is to "equip the saints" for ministry.
2. Discuss as a team and celebrate areas where people feel empowered and valued by the ministry leader or leaders.
3. Invite conversation from the volunteer leadership team and assess one or two ways or places where changes can be made to create a more collaborative team.
4. Commit to a specific plan with clear, measurable action steps to address the areas needing to change, and evaluate as you go.

Finding Partners among the Faithful

Once you embrace the partnering leadership model, you'll be surprised to see how many potential partners you can find in your own community if you open your eyes and your heart.

The partnering model sees the primary role of the leader as equipping the saints for the work of the ministry (Eph. 4:12). While appealing to unity in the body of gathered believers in Ephesus, the apostle Paul pointed out the reason that God has given certain primus leadership gifts in the body of siblings: "The gifts he gave were that some would be apostles, some prophets, some evangelists, some pastors and teachers, to equip the saints for the work of ministry, for building up the body of Christ, until all of us come to the unity of the faith and of the knowledge of the Son of God, to maturity, to the measure of the full stature of Christ" (Eph. 4:11–13 NRSV).

As Paul shows, the gifts of leadership are not given to control others, or to hoard ministry opportunities from others. It's not about me!

Paul's assignment to leaders is clear: "Equip the saints for the work of ministry." In the household of God, it is the body *as a whole* that does "the work of ministry, for building up the body of Christ."

As we saw in part 1, this kind of proactive partnering produces the kind of family and community that is whole and healthy enough to engage the world as agents of the kingdom of God. This, then, is the call of a partnering leader: to provide the kind of leadership where ministry partners are equipped to create an environment where adoptive youth ministry may thrive.

Many people may be considered partners in adoptive youth ministry, but three kinds of partners are most vital to your program's success: volunteers, non-volunteering adults, and parents. Let's look at these three populations as we explore what it means to design a strategy that equips all kinds of adults to play a part in the vital work of adoptive youth ministry.

Volunteers: The Core of a Partnering Ministry

Once you adopt a partnering model of ministry, you will need to identify and recruit volunteers who will work well in that model.

In his chapter on leadership in *Adoptive Youth Ministry*, Bill MacPhee describes the five commitments we must make in our efforts to bring on the best people to serve in the youth ministry: "We will be *selective*—since it is easier to hire than fire. We will be *protective*—of kids, other leaders, our own reputation and our church. We will be *direct*—by asking pointed questions as we pursue concerns. We will be *discerning*—by taking the time to evaluate motivation. We will be *clear*—by providing tangible steps for a potential volunteer to take in order to be on the team."[2] Here MacPhee raises the bar on the kinds of people we must seek out to serve in what he calls "direct ministry" roles involving regular relationships and relatively direct access to students.[3]

When we believe that someone, for whatever reason, may not be the best fit for a direct ministry role, a good alternative is to find a way that he or she can be involved in an indirect way, such as helping with ministry logistics (e.g., food, transportation, advocacy) or using their interests in supportive or background ways (like running a sound board or setting up a room). Determining what's best in each situation depends on interviews and conversation. Seek to discern what role might be the most satisfying and appropriate fit for any person who is interested in helping students on their journey into connection with God's household.

Recruiting the right volunteers—for either direct or indirect ministry—should remain a high priority for you in the role of partnering leader. They say it takes a village to raise a child. Likewise, it takes a dedicated group of direct and indirect ministry volunteers to facilitate an environment where students have the best chance to live into their mutual adoption in Christ among adult siblings as agents of the kingdom of God.

Equipping Volunteers

From the birth of the modern youth ministry era, volunteers have been front and center. Volunteers are those saints who perform roles for the benefit of others without being compensated. In theory, this means volunteers are committed to what they do because they sincerely want to help young people. For every cavalier volunteer who says, "Hey, I'm a volunteer! What are they going to do, *fire me?*" there are ten who are grateful for team members and leaders who love and support them.

I can't imagine what would happen to the world's churches and Christian organizations if all volunteers suddenly resigned en masse.

But it's a mistake to think of these saints as little more than a cheap way to get the job done.

Paul tells us that believers possess powerful spiritual gifts that can be used to build up the body of Christ. It's our job to equip the saints so they can use these gifts to their fullest in our ministries of partnership.

To maintain a focused commitment to a healthy, integrated adoptive ministry, each volunteer must be carefully recruited, vetted, equipped, and evaluated. The "any warm body will do" mentality from the previous era of youth ministry must be firmly put aside. The crucial role of direct ministry with youth requires the healthiest and best-trained members of your community. In a world where adolescents are surrounded by expectations, agendas, and abandonment, not just anyone can faithfully represent the body of Christ to them. Those who work on the front lines with the young deserve our dedication and investment in their success.

If you want your volunteers to succeed, they must buy in to and be accountable to the ministry's mission.

Quick, what's the mission of your ministry? If volunteers involved in direct ministry can't rattle off the correct answer, something is wrong.

Our mission is growing mature disciples of Jesus Christ. If volunteers don't grasp that and embrace it with all their hearts, they will fall into the common temptation of seeing youth ministry as little more than a series of fun—but ultimately empty—stand-alone events and experiences. Volunteers need to grasp how their ministry is a vital bridge linking committed, caring Christian adults to young people who desperately need what Christ and the church have to offer them.

That's why inviting, equipping, and encouraging men and women to nurture, serve, and empower students by playing the role of an adoptive mentor is one of the most vital aspects of adoptive youth ministry.

Training Volunteers

One of the biggest mistakes youth leaders make is recruiting great people and stopping there. But bringing people on board is only the beginning. It's your job to build up these members of the body for service. That's why volunteers and even staff need training.

Every single volunteer must be equipped to serve on your team, and each one deserves your best efforts at training—*both for their sake and for yours*. Training and equipping are related, but the former provides the skills needed to fulfill a role, while the latter imparts all that they need to be effective.

For direct ministry volunteers, training seems reasonable and obvious. Even with indirect volunteers, however, training is a way to encourage them to be more aware of the needs of students and the contextual intent of the ministry strategy and structure. More importantly, it is a way to possibly help move someone from an indirect role to a direct ministry role. So it is vital to train *all* volunteers.

That said, we must always remember that most people resist "training," especially if they have some experience. An axiom of ministry that must be emphasized in equipping volunteer leaders (and actually for any endeavor) is this: *Few people want to be trained, but everybody wants to be successful.*

Here is my rule, and I make it crystal clear: *All direct and indirect ministry volunteers must complete their initial training before I let them serve on the ministry's behalf.*

I also make sure that all volunteers fully understand and formally buy in to the ministry's core values and practices, including

- the purpose and goal of adoptive youth ministry;
- the current state of young people (culture, development, etc.);
- the particular contextualized strategy and structure of the local ministry;
- the role of a volunteer in that strategy; and
- the logistics of how the ministry functions (e.g., leader meetings, off-site events, legal issues like confidentiality and reporting regulations).

Train *before* Day One!

You have recruited a great group of volunteers. They are gung-ho to get going. But it's your job to stand up and say, "Great! I can't wait to get you involved in ministry to our youth. But first we need to complete your training!"

I have said that to parents before, and sometimes I've seen the blood draining out of their faces as they hear that dreaded word: *training*.

As the saying goes:

Few people want to be trained, but everybody wants to be successful.

But initial training is just the beginning. When you take on volunteers, you also take on the responsibility of continually building up these saints for their work by requiring them to participate in ongoing training. The purpose is twofold:

- Help them review and adhere to all ministry basics.
- Help them grow in their capacity for effective adoptive leadership.

The less your training sessions feel like training sessions, the better. Figure out what works best for your team, their needs, and the limitations of their time.

How and when you gather is something every group must decide so that people are neither unnecessarily burdened (e.g., busy people hating more meetings) nor excluded from serving because of their circumstances (such as a flight attendant or physician). Some groups have a monthly dinner and time for "team building" on Sunday nights. Other groups gather mini-teams (like the small group leaders, or program and worship leaders) monthly or every other week for forty-five minutes to explore topics relevant to their roles, and then gather quarterly with the entire team for more in-depth, corporate, Christ-centered community building, training, and prayer.

The important thing to remember is that every ministry team member *must* be trained, with at least the following four components as guidance every time you gather:

1. *Building the team in unity as followers of Jesus Christ.* This generally includes corporate spiritual practices such as prayer, praise, singing, Scripture, and meditation. The key is to make sure the team is consistently focused on being the people of God as they do the work of God.

2. *Connecting with and understanding students.* In the initiation training phase, the basics of child and adolescent development, cultural awareness, and family dynamics and influence should be presented. With ongoing training, every volunteer should be given the opportunity to go deeper into any of these and related issues in a way that is immediately applicable.

3. *Providing a sense of ownership in the ministry.* Most volunteers feel disconnected from the decision-making process of ministry, and this is a recipe for discouragement, burnout, and volunteer turnover. As primus (the first among equals), the leader must make sure that all relevant players have some say about what goes on in the ministry. Numerous things could be discussed. A change in camp venue, a mission trip schedule, or a shift in programmatic structure are but a sample of what a team needs to not only know about but also engage in determining so that everyone feels they are important to the team.

4. *Encouraging the team.* As Paul exhorts in 1 Thessalonians, "Encourage one another and build each other up" (5:11). To encourage people may be the most affectively important element of volunteer training. Volunteers often feel disconnected, neglected, used, and, most of all, discouraged. Encouragement can take a variety of forms, and this is where you can be your most creative self: provide coffee shop gift cards for everyone, buy them an uplifting book, give volunteers a kind mention

from up front. These are but a few of the ways to make people feel like the church and leadership actually *care* about the volunteers who are so invested.

4 Key Ministry Training Components

1. Building growth and unity in Christ
2. Understanding students
3. Providing ownership for the ministry
4. Creating an environment of encouragement

Recruiting Other Adults in Your Community through VAST

I have witnessed too many youth workers like Rich who can't stop grumbling about how nobody in their church understands or cares about kids. I pray that these leaders will open their eyes and ask God to guide them to those men and women in the community who have a passion for youth ministry but, for one reason or another, don't volunteer.

These people are an essential part of your team, for they can be a part of your vision and support team (VAST).

A VAST can be composed of a small trusted group or as many adults as you can possibly gather in a room. All must be deeply invested in and committed to the ministry. Some may be parents, but this is not a parent council (see below on partnering with parents). Some may be active in the youth ministry, at least on the periphery, but this is not a typical leadership group.

The best VASTs that I have seen are made up of former volunteer youth workers, a handful of parents whose oldest children are either nearing graduation or still in elementary school, and a few other adults who care about the nurture of students.

If your church has a board (or the equivalent), then you might have one or more board members join, but a VAST should not be an officially designated "committee" under the direction of the board (many churches have an elder board or maybe a personnel committee who serve as lay supervisors over youth ministry; the VAST does not function in this way, as they are there to *partner* with the leadership of the ministry and not supervise).

A VAST has two basic functions: vision and support.

Vision

The job description of the VAST is to provide partnership for the vision and overarching planning of the adoptive ministry. It is a mini-community whose members don't appear on any official flowchart but do carry influence through relationship, commitment, and knowledge of the ministry's goal and contextualized strategy.

The VAST must not only be clear in their articulation of adoptive youth ministry as applied in their setting; they must also know why and how the ministry strategy and structure seek to accomplish the goal of an organic adoptive ministry. All conversations and deliberations that a VAST and a ministry team have should remain fixed on the call of God to living out mutual adoption and the overall goal of how youth ministry encourages and creates the environment for it.

The role of vision, then, is less about where or when to go to camp or on a mission trip, and more about why and how a camp or mission experience fits the call and goal.

Support

While the vision role of the VAST is strategically and structurally important, support is equally valuable. You need a group of invested lay adults who are committed to supporting not only the work of the ministry (flipping burgers or driving vans) but also the efforts and people of the ministry.

Whenever a former student contacts me, asking me how to handle a certain ministry situation involving church politics or relationship issues, the first question I ask is, "What does your VAST have to say about this?" The overwhelming majority of the time, the person responds, "Um, remind me: What is a VAST again? I know it was on the final, but . . ." What I haven't found surprising is that when I hear from a former student who *has* implemented a VAST-type group to partner with, almost every conversation is about how loved and supported they feel and how well their ministry is going.

An example of how this plays out came in an email from a former student: "Thought you'd like to see this agenda—the VAST is the best advice you gave me when I took the job. They keep me on my toes, but it is awesome to have their input." He sent me this email that his VAST chair sent to the team, summarizing their recent meeting (I have included an excerpt):

Hi VASTeam,

I hope you all are having a good day. We missed some of you yesterday at the VAST meeting, but I'm sending you what was discussed yesterday.

1. LA Mission Trip

    a. We have 15 kids currently signed up, but would love for more as the Lord leads. Any ideas, please let us know.

2. Jennifer's Goodbye Party is this Saturday, May 13 at 6 PM at the Farmers'. Tacos are provided ($5 suggested donation); bring a side dish.

3. Memorial Weekend Mexico Trip

    a. Sarah and Jim will not be going because they'll be home with the new baby.

    b. As we think about this trip in the future, what are ways to connect adults with kids more?

4. Adoption Task Force—how can we get more adults at our church to invest in the lives of students?

a. An idea the staff has: Ask 5–6 adults in the church to get to know specific kids whose names we will give them.

b. Missional Communities have been making an impact by bringing kids and adults together.

c. VAST idea: Adults vs. Kids (or half and half) in a kickball or softball tournament during the summer. We will discuss this next week.

VAST: From Concept to Action

Your VAST should have a chair (or perhaps cochairs) who is in regular contact with the ministry leader. This relationship between the ministry and VAST leadership is key to the work of the team.

Chairs are co-mentors with the youth director, and the mutuality of the relationship they share goes well beyond the "business" of ministry and includes their personal and spiritual journeys and, when appropriate, their personal lives. In partnership, the VAST chair (or chairs) and the director are committed not just to the adoptive ministry but also to the health and welfare of the staff and volunteers.

To be effective, VASTs should meet regularly, perhaps once a month. They should be committed to pray for the people and the ministry and, where it is organic and fits, see their role outside of meetings as holding a place between the congregation, board, ministry leadership, and students and their families. They are the lay team that functions as the "equals" the primus works with for vision and support.

Recruiting and Building Up Parents

You may not be aware that equipping parents for ministry to their children is part of your job, but it is!

There are two ways youth workers typically view parents. One way strengthens the ministry. The other way weakens it. Which way do you want to go?

Parents Are the Problem

I've heard it expressed in a million ways:

- What is it with these parents?
- Why are their kids such jerks?
- How could they fail so miserably in giving their kids a basic foundation in the faith?

I heard it once in the parking lot of a large church where I served as a consulting supervisor of the youth staff. I was huddled with a group of middle school students getting ready to board a bus for a worship night at a local theme park. The youth leader, who had failed to give the parents any written information about the event, gave three curious final pieces of information:

- He informed parents he had taken the students' cell phones so they wouldn't be distracted during the event (he would give them back to the students when they arrived back at the church).
- He warned them how important it was for parents not to be late when the bus arrived (ETA 1:30 a.m.).
- He gave out his cell number but instructed the parents "not to call me unless it is an emergency, because there are too many of you, so please be early and wait for us."

One mother expressed her problems with this arrangement. She introduced herself as a single mom who was new to the church and whose sixth-grade daughter was going on her first trip. She wanted him to know to watch out for her daughter.

Then she said, "And I also have a six-year-old who is in the car now who is pretty sick, and I don't have access to a sitter. Would you mind helping me get my daughter a ride home?"

Just as the youth leader was about to respond, his wife came out from behind him and told the woman, "Do you realize what you are asking of us? Do you see how many kids are here? We are only responsible to take your child to and from the event, *not* to find her a ride. There is no way we can do that."

Then the youth leader and his wife walked away.

I watched the mom, all alone, wandering aimlessly and looking for someone to give her daughter a ride home. One couple who was going on the trip had overheard the exchange and offered to take care of her daughter while there and drive her home. But the damage was done. The mother left visibly dejected.

When the middle school pastor and I met the next week, I began by inviting him to debrief about this event. He didn't mention the encounter with the mom, so I did it for him, asking about the exchange. Thirty seconds later, he said what was on his heart: "Entitled parents in this church are constantly asking for favors from me, and that's not my job!"

Two months later he found a new job. In his exit interview he said he was leaving to go where, he told me, "he would be appreciated for his years of experience."

Parents Are Partners

How could the encounter with the mom in the parking lot have gone differently?

The youth leader could have provided parents with the information they needed in advance. He could have started the evening by thanking the parents for their support and for bringing their children to participate in the evening. When the mother approached him, he could have said, "I understand and will do everything I can to help you get this solved." And instead of walking away, he could have welcomed the mother's daughter, who suddenly felt uncomfortable about all the attention.

Parents can be your best partners if you work with them. First, parents will *feel* like partners if we would but come alongside them, get to know them, and encourage them. In addition, every person who is building an adoptive church ministry should see every parent as a resource into what is best not only for their child but for others as well. There are many simple ways we can help parents to know that we want and need them as our ministry partners, but in my experience this has for some reason been seen as a difficult and even unnecessary part of our role. But no one knows a child better than that child's parents! It seems like a simple idea, but it's crucial in setting parents' minds at ease when they're handing their precious children off to you.

Parents wonder if anyone in your ministry cares about their child even remotely as much as they do. When you represent an adoptive ministry church, where every child is cared for and valued, you can help parents know that you want to walk with them as you lead and love their children. This is especially true for those parents who do not attend your church.

Harnessing the Power of Partnership

Rich's story didn't end that day in the restaurant. He was let go, went to work for a local coffee shop, and started to go to a church where they didn't know he had been in a prominent youth ministry position. He stayed close to his Christian friends, and he and I met monthly mostly so that I could encourage him to keep thinking, growing, and praying. His anger began to melt, and his heart stayed soft toward Christ and his kingdom.

This led to conversations with me and others exploring with Rich what he had learned from his experience. He came to see that in his enthusiasm and his perception of his abilities, he had denied others access to ministry. His own father was a dominant leader, and he came to see that his greatest struggle was to prove himself. Rich wanted to make sure people valued him; he just couldn't let others succeed. Eventually he grew to the point where he could reengage in ministry, and he found another position where he could try out his new collaborative wings. Rich is still in ministry, grown up as a man and leader, with a solid team walking beside him.

The role of a leader, especially in an adoptive ministry context, is "to equip [Christ's] people for works of service, so that the body of Christ may be built up" (Eph. 4:12). This takes a primus leader who embraces the power of partnership.

8

Building Your Ministry Team

The four Gospels show us the person, character, and work of Jesus, while the book of Acts shows how the newly instituted group of people known as "the church" lived out the calling of Christ.

Sometimes things went great, as we see from these verses in Acts 2:

> They devoted themselves to the apostles' teaching and to fellowship, to the breaking of bread and to prayer. Everyone was filled with awe at the many wonders and signs performed by the apostles. All the believers were together and had everything in common. They sold property and possessions to give to anyone who had need. Every day they continued to meet together in the temple courts. They broke bread in their homes and ate together with glad and sincere hearts, praising God and enjoying the favor of all the people. And the Lord added to their number daily those who were being saved. (vv. 42–47)

Other times things weren't so great. Factions began to develop in some of the earliest churches. Some believers thought the congregation should do one thing, while another group felt they should do the opposite.

As we read Paul's letters to various churches, we can see him constantly trying to encourage believers to embrace unity over disunity. Often Paul's pleas for brotherly love circled back to where it all began: the believers' mutual adoption in Christ. Like a stern but loving father, Paul attempted to reason with his quarrelsome children.

Listen, he said. Once upon a time each and every one of us was lost in our sin and selfishness and alienated from our Creator God. But then Jesus came along, adopting all of us spiritual orphans and lovingly placing us in a brand-new family made up of fellow brothers and sisters in Christ.

So, Paul asked, why do we want to act like we acted before we knew Christ and were transformed by the Holy Spirit? Why are we sacrificing the unity of the body of Christ over squabbles concerning who has the greater status, which teachers are the best, which spiritual gifts are most important? (See Galatians 4 and Ephesians 1 where he makes these points.)

Members of the various churches were trying to settle issues using the same tough tactics that had worked for them in their business lives or in conflicts with neighbors. Paul said there must be a better way. In 1 Corinthians 12 he explains how the body should function:

- "The body is made up of not one part but many" (v. 14).
- "God has placed the parts in the body, every one of them, just as he wanted them to be. . . . Giving greater honor to the parts that lacked it, so that there should be no division in the body, but that its parts should have equal concern for each other" (vv. 18, 24–25).
- "Now you are the body of Christ, and each one of you is a part of it" (v. 27).

Paul's message is clear: We believers are a body, a household of siblings where each member is equally valued. Therefore, we must function as a body. Every member is called. Every member is gifted. Every person has talents to offer. Every person is necessary to the healthy functioning of the body.

I call this a "theology of team." But it seems that the corporate world often understands the team concept much better than Christian leaders do. As I will demonstrate in the following pages, your calling as the leader of an adoptive youth ministry is not to be a manager producing results but to be a leader who produces people who produce results. You can grow this kind of dynamic team if you want to.

The Eight Essentials of Effective Teams

Carl Larson and Frank LaFasto are business leaders and consultants who spent three years finding out how teams work. They studied successful corporations, NASA, Notre Dame's 1966 championship football team, and the five-thousand-person crew serving on the supercarrier USS *Kitty Hawk*. They published their results in their 1989 book, *Teamwork: What Must Go Right, What Can Go Wrong*.[1] Eight characteristics inspired by their research can help strengthen our own ministry teams.

A Clear, Elevating Goal

Larson and LaFasto argue that a clear, elevating goal is the single most important characteristic of effective teams. In cases where the goal is not clear, different people have different ideas and objectives, leading to conflict and disunity within the team.

Eight Essentials of Effective Teams

1. A clear, elevating goal
2. A results-driven structure
3. Competent team members
4. Unified commitment
5. A collaborative climate
6. Standards of excellence
7. External support and recognition
8. Principled leadership

Mundane, ho-hum goals are not sufficient. In order for people to rally around it, a goal must be clear and compelling enough to hold the team members' attention and inspire their excitement and commitment. In effective teams, not only does each member know and articulate the collective goal, but each member also knows deep down that the goal matters.

The goal of adoptive youth ministry is both clear and elevating. Our purpose is not to invite individual young people to make individual decisions about their individual spiritual lives. When we align our lives with Christ, we find ourselves in a new family where we can experience a sense of community, connectedness, unity, and teamwork that eluded us prior to coming to faith.

Unfortunately, the history of youth ministry in America has focused more on individualism than unity or community. In part, that's because our youth work forefathers largely embraced the model of the tent revival, where each person is called to make a decision for Christ. This individual invitation to faith overflows into our individual approach to discipleship. Our culture's value of rugged individualism outweighs the biblical mandate for unity within the body.

In youth ministry, this individualism manifests itself in believers who say, "I'm on my own to fulfill the calling that I have in Christ." Our appeals to students are often based on personal faith and piety, not adoption into the community of believers.

You and your coworkers can successfully override these cultural currents if you commit yourself to creating a team where your goal of adoptive youth ministry is crystal clear to each and every person—from the youth leader to direct ministry volunteer to indirect ministry volunteer.

And how do you know if your team members are on board with the goal? Ask them. It's amazing how raising questions about our core ministry goal—our reason for doing ministry in the first place—can bring clarity and resolve to discussions where people seem to have different ideas about what to do.

Your job is to make sure that every small group leader, the person who sets up the chairs, the guy who flips burgers, and the woman who drives the van to the mission trip can state the mission of adoptive youth ministry with precision (clear) and enthusiasm (elevating).

To repeat, this is the goal we have been working from:

> The goal of adoptive youth ministry is to create an environment where young people are encouraged to live into their calling in Christ as agents of the kingdom within the household of God.

Leaders must ensure that this ministry goal is clearly communicated, understood, and wholeheartedly embraced by all members of the team. This won't happen in a day. It requires a long-term commitment and regular coaching to make sure everyone gets on—and stays on—the same page.

I've personally seen how a clear and compelling goal can revolutionize youth ministries and empower everyone involved to promote the group's shared vision. You will know you have arrived when the person who sweeps the floors is convinced that clean floors support an environment where students may encounter Christ alongside their spiritual siblings; when parents who sign up for the prayer ministry feel connected to the goal and can contribute through this powerful form of indirect ministry; and when team meetings are punctuated by various members quoting the goal and strategizing how to most effectively reach it.

It's not enough that you and a handful of the most faithful volunteers know the goal. Your job is to train each and every member of your team to see that their role in the work is just as essential as that done by all the other fellow agents of the kingdom of God.

We'll finish our look at a clear, elevating goal (as we will for each of the characteristics of effective teams) by summarizing the key elements (the *dos*, the *don'ts*, and the *must*) of this essential characteristic.

The **Dos** of a Clear, Elevating Goal

- Train it.
- Print it.
- Talk often about it.
- Remind each other about it.
- Evaluate everything you do in light of it.
- Pray together for it.

The **Don'ts** of a Clear, Elevating Goal

- Ignore it when it's violated.
- Allow it to be less important than numbers, success, or something that "works."

The **Must** of a Clear, Elevating Goal

Everyone on the team must know, believe in, and commit to this purpose.

A Results-Driven Structure

With the goal clearly in mind, you're ready to focus on the structure of your adoptive youth ministry. But remember, your assignment as a leader is not to *do* everything that needs to be done, but to encourage and enable the team that will make it happen.

It's amazing what a community focused on a single goal can achieve when they know that everything they do is pointing in the same direction. For one thing, you can stop focusing on programs and activities as ends in themselves and begin seeing them as steps toward achieving your ministry's goals. For example:

- We play games not to fill time before our meeting ends but to build trust among students and between students and leaders.
- We teach theological content not so students can win a Bible quiz or demonstrate their mastery of Scripture but to help them better understand the love of Christ.
- We meet with students in small groups not just because it's a convenient alternative to large group gatherings but because students need to know what it looks like to experience intimate relationships in Christ with others.

I'm not proposing you set fire to your library of games and activities, but rather that you use adoptive youth ministry to help determine which of these activities will actually help you reach your goal and which activities will hinder your progress.

The **Dos** of a Results-Driven Structure

- Design everything you do with the aim of achieving the goal of adoptive youth ministry.
- Ensure that everyone on the team knows *how* what you do directly points toward that goal.
- Create an atmosphere where hard questions are invited to help keep the team on course.

The **Don'ts** of a Results-Driven Structure

- Plan or program anything that does not point toward the goal.
- Assume or expect the team to know *how* what you do points toward the goal.
- Allow an attitude of defensiveness when the team lacks clarity of purpose for what you do.

The **Must** of a Results-Driven Structure

Everyone on the team must see how everything they do points in the direction of the goal of adoptive youth ministry.

Competent Team Members

Research shows that leaders typically believe they are doing a better job of helping team members excel than they actually are. That's too bad, because one of your most important tasks as a leader is to make sure all the people on your team are maximizing their callings. Larson and LaFasto warn about these blind spots among team leaders: "The most severe complaint about team leadership from team members involves leaders who are unwilling to confront and resolve issues associated with an adequate performance by team members. Leaders see themselves as far more active in this area than do team members."[2]

Let's use football to illustrate the point. You're the coach of a team, and all your players are committed to all eight of the team characteristics. But you'll never win any games without a quarterback to throw passes, or without a left tackle to keep pass rushers from gang-tackling your quarterback. You need competent team members to fill these positions if you want to succeed and win.

So how do you translate this model from the football field to adoptive youth ministry? You need to make sure your team members are well suited to and capable in the roles they take on. For me, this includes basic functional competency in their area of service as well as factors like self-awareness and Christian commitment.

For example, how do you recruit competent small group leaders? Everyone who expresses a willingness to be a part of your team deserves the opportunity to work with leadership and see if their callings to serve match the ministry's needs and expectations. Hopefully, you can place every competent volunteer in a role that fits his or her gifts and talents.

Ideally, you want to fill every role with good volunteers, but what happens if you experience a personnel shortfall? That's where you have to make changes. Perhaps one year your ministry offers your students four small groups (for boys and girls of different ages), but the next year you can only staff two small groups. One way to address this is to offer small groups in the fall for the girls and in the spring for the guys. That would be better than keeping all four groups but having some led by people who are not competent to do so.

Helping people find a place to serve that matches their gifts is a wonderful experience, but your duty does not stop there. You must regularly train them (see chap. 7) to help them reach their full effectiveness. In doing so, you will help them grow in competency, which helps your team reach its goal.

The **Dos** of Having Competent Team Members

- Provide anyone who demonstrates a sincere faith and a genuine love for young people a place on the team (this may be in direct or indirect ministry).
- Insist on initiation and regular, ongoing training for *all* team members.
- Consistently remind each other that everyone is welcome at the table to care for the young.
- Create a climate of evaluation where the goal is to find the right spot for each team member, and structure accordingly.

The **Don'ts** of Having Competent Team Members

- Assume that people understand the basic elements of adoptive youth ministry.
- Assume that people know how to use their gifts and talents in ministry to young people.
- Create a structure where people feel like they are filling programmatic slots rather than freely engaging students.

- Reserve all or most of the up-front opportunities for team leaders or a select few.
- Make training rote, boring, or mechanical.

The **Must** of Having Competent Team Members

A team leader's primary role is to help others who are called to the team to succeed.

Unified Commitment

When some leaders try to ascertain the commitment level of their team members, they adopt a simple metric: commitment is revealed when people show up and do the work, and those who don't show up don't care.

This is sometimes the case, but it's far from a rule. People in your congregation have a variety of responsibilities. Some are in demanding professional careers. Some have children with special needs or are caring for ailing parents. Others have bad bosses who demand they work overtime without any warning. These busy people may care about your ministry but lack the freedom to be as involved as they would like to be. Please don't make the mistake of prematurely writing off these valuable people.

Time is an important factor in measuring commitment, but I think it's better to measure commitment by understanding people's determination and heart. One volunteer may be retired and have extra time on his hands, allowing him to attend every single leader meeting you schedule. Another volunteer may show up late to events or programs, or even cancel at the last minute. Understandably, these kinds of scenarios can drive a wedge between team members. The consistent volunteers may even resent those they see as less committed, leading to anger and bitterness. But those who can't attend—because they've been called out of town, or the boss just demanded more work—may actually be more committed to your team's adoptive ministry goal than the ones who are there regularly.

Your role as the leader is to help potential volunteers discern what kind of involvement is reasonable. A flight attendant, police officer, or high school teacher who is also a referee should never be excluded from direct ministry simply because they may have to be late or miss meetings and events. The key to avoiding conflict is to make sure that people's schedules and commitment are known and even celebrated team-wide.

It takes all kinds of saints to build relational bridges with the various young people in your ministry. And students generally care less about a person's schedule than they care about a person's willful commitment to them. Students can tell the difference between someone who truly cares and someone who is just along for the ride.

The **Dos** of Unified Commitment

- Build an atmosphere where all who are committed are invited to serve as they are able.
- Allow for unique job descriptions to match people's lives and livelihoods.
- Facilitate open dialogue so that everyone on the team is aware of others' needs and schedules and is encouraged to be there for one another as team members.
- Pray to the "Lord of the harvest" for a variety of people to join the team (Matt. 9:38).

The **Don'ts** of Unified Commitment

- "Recruit" volunteers primarily out of programmatic necessity.
- Ask for too much or too little from the team as you work together to create job descriptions.

- Create artificial limitations for people who have irregular schedules.

The **Must** of Unified Commitment

Since "health breeds health" and people want to be a part of something where they are valued and encouraged, create a family-like leadership team and ethos to foster an environment where adoptive youth ministry can flourish.

A Collaborative Climate

What does it mean to collaborate? A few simple illustrations will paint a clearer picture than a dictionary definition.

When I am dancing a slow dance with my wife, she and I collaborate by moving together instead of each of us moving separately. If we're successful, we experience a oneness as we move together.

When I am working on an article or a book with another leader, we collaborate by sharing our ideas freely and seeing which ones make the most sense to the most youth workers instead of duking it out for control or dominance.

Collaboration is actually at the heart of all ministry, because nothing takes place unless we collaborate with the Holy Spirit in what we do. And it is especially crucial as we try to build an adoptive youth ministry.

In my experience, collaboration in youth ministry is often more about the feel or spirit of a team than the logistics involved in doing a particular task. Team members need to feel that they are working together in unity to achieve shared ministry goals. They need to "be" as a team before they "do" the team's work. Another way to say it is this: we are called to be the people of God before we do the work of God.

What does it take to be a collaborative team member, and how can a leader foster collaboration in ministry? This can be challenging, because some people will be more naturally committed to a collaborative way of working than others. As Larson and LaFasto say, "The attitudes, styles, and interaction patterns of team members have a direct impact on performance outcomes."[3] (The authors' "Collaborative Team Member rating sheet"[4] provides a helpful tool for evaluating team members' willingness and ability to work with others on the team.)

In some cases, collaboration is a function of personality type. People who are open, supportive, and generally positive are typically more willing to work collaboratively than those who are closed, unsupportive, and negative. Training can help Lone Rangers adopt a more collaborative approach, but this doesn't work with everyone. When I encounter a person who has difficulty collaborating, I find a different role for them that requires less teamwork.

Your role in adoptive youth ministry is about environment as much as it is about "production" or "effectiveness." Your willingness to serve others instead of ruling over them will go a long way toward creating the kind of dynamic spiritual climate that is magnetic to both volunteers and students.

Collaboration is important in many settings, but it's essential when your goal is adoptive youth ministry. Our goal is clear and direct: to create an environment where adolescents are encouraged to live into their mutual adoption in Christ as siblings in the household of faith as agents of the kingdom.

> "We are called to be the people of God before we do the work of God."

If you can create a collaborative climate where all members are committed to modeling spiritual unity, the impact your volunteers have will be magnified many times.

The **Dos** of Creating a Collaborative Climate

- Make healthy relationships on the team a primary commitment. Seek to be the people of God *before* you do the work of God.
- Create an atmosphere of honest communication and short relational accounts, where conflicts are addressed kindly and quickly ("speaking the truth in love" [Eph. 4:15]).
- Provide a sense of ownership for all members of the team.
- Worship often with each other.
- Pray *and play* together as a team.

The **Don'ts** of Creating a Collaborative Climate

- Allow factions among team members to take root.
- Play favorites or encourage only the more "gifted."
- Allow people to feel like they are volunteers who are serving the leader, as opposed to corporately serving the Lord in leading and loving the young.
- Ignore contentious or disruptive behavior of a member.

The **Must** of Creating a Collaborative Climate

Since modeling family relationships is an essential aspect of adoptive youth ministry, ensure that the youth ministry team likes being and serving together like a family.

Standards of Excellence

If you are a salesperson, your goal is clear: make more sales. If you play soccer, your goal is to score more points and block more shots.

But a salesperson who arrives late for work, doesn't keep accurate records, or doesn't return phone calls will not succeed at his job. And a college athlete who ignores off-season workouts, eats poorly, and takes shortcuts in practice will eventually find herself cut from the team. That's why successful companies and teams require a basic commitment to standards of excellence that match the task at hand.

Those of us who minister to young people have embraced a high calling that comes with high standards and expectations. The apostle Paul made this clear in a series of pastoral letters that spell out the high standards of excellence required of all servants of the gospel. Paul frequently offered his own life as a model that other leaders should emulate: "You are witnesses, and so is God, of how holy, righteous and blameless we were among you who believed. For you know that we dealt with each of you as a father deals with his own children, encouraging, comforting and urging you to live lives worthy of God, who calls you into his kingdom and glory" (1 Thess. 2:10–12).

In academic circles, there is much hand-wringing about how to discuss standards of excellence, as one journal article explained: "Because it lacks content, 'excellence' serves in the broadest sense solely as an (aspirational) claim of comparative success: that some thing, person, activity, or institution can be asserted in a hopefully convincing fashion to be 'better' or 'more important' than some other (often otherwise incomparable) thing, person, activity, or institution—and, crucially, that it is, as a result, more deserving of reward. But this emphasis on reward is itself often poisonous to the actual qualities of the underlying activity."[5]

In youth ministry settings, excellence should not become elitism. We are not separating sheep from goats here, but merely seeking to have the right people in the right spots.

As a ministry leader, you are not setting yourself apart from others but identifying with them as a fellow sinner saved by grace, and a fellow child of God who is grateful that God saw fit to adopt *you* into his family. You are modeling, in essence, what you are trying to elicit from your church community in adoptive youth ministry.

You do not want to send the exclusionary message that some people aren't qualified to be involved in the ministry. It's better to say, "Come one, come all, and we'll get you started with our mandatory training that will help get you up to speed on our standards and practices."

You never know who will answer the call. Nancy, a seventy-seven-year-old at a church I have been working with, offered to "help out with the kids," and soon she was thrust into the role of a small group leader of eleventh- and twelfth-grade girls. After several months she confided in me, "I haven't changed them, they've changed me!" The young women Nancy works with say the same thing. "Nancy has been such a gift to us," one shared with me. "She loves us as we are, and she doesn't throw advice at us or talk down to us, but treats us like we have something to offer her."

As an adoptive youth ministry leader, your standards of excellence should focus on two things:

- getting the right people in the right spots; and
- training, coaching, mentoring, and developing these people who approach ministry out of a sincere reverence for and obedience to Jesus Christ but may lack a few skills.

By committing yourself to this kind of leadership, you are probably doing something for your kids that's way more important than any single lesson you have ever taught. You're displaying what it really looks like to practice full inclusion among all of us siblings in God's amazing kingdom.

The **Dos** of Standards of Excellence

- From the outset, ensure that every team member is committed to growing as a follower of Christ *aside from the youth ministry community.*
- Be diligent as a team that everything that is done is well prepared and well delivered.

- With people who are trying out new opportunities or ministry roles, train in advance, observe during, and meet following to evaluate and sharpen so that they may grow and be successful.
- Require that all team members are committed to the local body (the church) as much as they are to the youth ministry or students (adoptive ministry cannot work without this).

The **Don'ts** of Standards of Excellence

- Allow the "doing" of tasks to be the center or reason for ministry.
- Ignore sloppy or lack of preparation.
- Settle for second best in terms of ministry, especially direct ministry, unless there is a deliberative commitment to training the novices.
- Look away from indicators that team members are not nurturing their own faith.

The **Must** of Standards of Excellence

Team leadership must be more concerned with encouraging people to grow in their authentic walk with Christ than with running the program.

External Support and Recognition

When volunteers become frustrated, there are two things you will hear them say:

- "I'm not really making a difference in anybody's life."
- "Nobody really seems to care what I'm doing here."

When I hear volunteers say these things, it typically means they are not getting the support and encouragement they need to thrive in their ministerial roles.

When team members feel supported and encouraged, it's far easier for them to believe that they are making an impact. But when they don't get that encouragement, their spirits weaken and their confidence sinks.

Larson and LaFasto's research in the business world revealed that even sky-high salaries aren't enough to soothe the souls of corporate titans who are discouraged about the impact or significance of their work.

I've seen it myself. People may have a strong inner sense of purpose and calling when they first volunteer to join your team, but the strength of that passion wanes when challenges set in and the personal payoffs seem lower than anticipated.

God has designed us to want to be in the game, to matter, and to make a difference. Positive psychology refers to this as discovering one's purpose. But without external support and recognition, that purpose can erode into self-defeat and discouragement. Even the most faithful volunteer or staff person needs a healthy dose of both support and recognition in order to stay the course in ministry.

I suspect some readers may be getting nervous at this point. Relax! Don't think of support and encouragement as something new to add to your endless list of duties. Rather, embrace it as a foundational part of your ongoing relationship with and training of your team members.

Think of support as the ongoing work of making sure a team member knows that they have the team—and especially church leaders—on their side. If they need something, there will be a way to find it. When they feel like they are ill-equipped for a given situation or issue, then the team has both the resources and the will to ensure that the person gets what they need.

Far too often, once the initial training and structure have been implemented, support falls off the leadership's radar. One strategy for providing the necessary support is to enlist an indirect ministry team whose job is to provide support to the direct ministry volunteers on a consistent basis. As we saw in chapter 7, a ministry that creates a vision and support structure can provide an ideal vehicle for this type of service.

How you do it is up to you, whether specific team members are given this responsibility or a team leader builds a mutual support system among team members. Either way, it is essential that every team member feels supported by the whole and by the leader, who is ultimately responsible for the morale of the team.

But don't stop there. Adults who give themselves away in the service of young people deserve—and often need—strong and regular doses of external recognition. Some leaders do this at an annual "volunteer banquet." Others recognize volunteers during a worship service at the end of the year. And while general public expressions of appreciation are fine, we can go further in encouraging and supporting our volunteers.

In a healthy family, members encourage one another when they see someone is hurting or needs an emotional lift. That's what an adoptive church does in the household of God. In ministry it is all too easy to focus on the tasks that we do in ministry rather than fostering adoptive community family-like care. A harried single mother may need an extra measure of care, and when a volunteer goes out of her way to step in, leadership should do our best not only to encourage that volunteer's commitment but also to acknowledge that this kind of service is what ministry is about.

Instead of handing out plaques, have appreciative church members tell personal stories of how they saw each individual team member play a valuable role in a teen's life. Have leaders stop by a volunteer or small group meeting just to say thank you to the team member. Send someone an email, thanking them for the specific spiritual gift they bring to the body.

The key is to support and encourage team members in ways that are specific and clear so they know someone notices and appreciates all their work and effort.

The Dos of External Support and Recognition

- Make being on the team an opportunity for fun and celebration.

- Spend time on a volunteer's turf, ensuring that each one knows that they are valuable as people and not just as servants to the ministry program.
- Budget and plan for formal and informal expressions of gratitude and thanks.
- Be extravagant with affirmation (e.g., for those who have children, offer free babysitting for non-church events; for those who don't, find other tangible ways to express gratitude and affirmation—such as giving gift cards to a volunteer's favorite specialty store or local restaurant).

The **Don'ts** of External Support and Recognition

- Communicate that a member's value is in proportion to their service to the ministry.
- Allow support and recognition to be superficial or generic.

The **Must** of External Support and Recognition

The team leadership must ensure that every member knows that they matter as a *person* more than as a *leader*.

Principled Leadership

For a team to function well, members must trust their leader. This is so foundational that it should hardly need mentioning, but unfortunately many of us know from personal experience that it *does* need mentioning.

So what does "principled leadership" look like in practice? I consider three things essential.

First, a ministry team leader must treat others in a way that aligns with the message we proclaim. In adoptive youth ministry, where the entire emphasis is family-like relationships among equally valued siblings, a leader who treats people like they are tools or pawns on a chessboard undercuts the theological foundations of the ministry.

When each team member is treated as a called and gifted peer, students see what kinds of relationships they can expect in the church at large. But when students see leaders take advantage of others or exploit their power, the game is up. Our words matter, but our actions speak much louder.

Second, we ministry leaders must seek consistency in how our personal faith affects and informs our daily living. There must be alignment between what we say and how we live if we expect students and volunteers to place confidence in us as trustworthy and reliable guides on the journey of faith.

I have used the words *consistency* and *alignment*, but young people have their own word for people who do what I'm talking about: authenticity.

Some leaders project that they are wise in all things and utterly invincible, which can make them seem unapproachable. Others project that they are weak and uncertain and beset by constant sins and temptations, which makes them seem just like the kids. Why would kids trust that person? For many young people today, authenticity is a high value. But they also want adults in their lives who, while honest about their real life struggles, also have the ability to move through their circumstances with hope and faith. The rule of thumb, then, for those of us serving adolescents relationally is to offer ourselves as a friend on a journey without inviting young people into our current or habitual struggles. Some adults have used kids as best friends or even confidants. But kids have enough to worry about for themselves, and this is the last thing they need from someone in a leadership role. Instead, we need to find our own safe places to wrestle with the difficult struggles of life and faith.

And above all, if you (or anyone else on the team) have lost your spiritual footing, or become involved in immorality, or for some reason lost faith in Christ, you must be honest enough to step away from the leadership role, if even for just a season.

Third, while we must be deadly serious about our responsibility as leaders, we must remain approachable and teachable. Being open to helpful and respectful critique, offering a spirit of collegial friendship to one another (and students), and seeking to be connected with team members beyond the ministry roles we play will all go a long way in creating a sense that the leader can be trusted.

The **Dos** of Principled Leadership

- Model authentic faith and integrity.
- Invite the team to share their lives with one another, not just "do ministry" together.
- Admit wrong and ask forgiveness.
- Seek to be gracious when others fail.
- Pray together often as a team.

The **Don'ts** of Principled Leadership

- Create an atmosphere where only the leader's opinion matters.
- Function only as a task-oriented team.
- Talk more than listen.

The **Must** of Principled Leadership

The team leader must be a person who leads as the first among equals who encourages the inherent worth of each team member.

Building the Ministry Team

It takes a commitment to strategic thinking to facilitate an adoptive ministry and to create the kind of environment where young people feel nurtured, empowered, and included. For adoptive ministry to take hold, how you put the pieces together to implement your vision is crucial. First, it is important to create your ministry based on your context (chap. 6). Second, you will gather around you ministry partners who are committed and trained to flesh out your goal (chap. 7). Finally, your work is to build a team of people who will represent Jesus Christ and the local community in relationship with students and young adults. This chapter is about that team, making sure that everyone is on the same page with the style and end goal of everything that happens in the name of ministry. Each person, whether their role is visible or background, small or large, is a crucial link in helping a young person make the transition from the isolating world of adolescence and emerging adulthood into the family-like community of God's household. Taking each volunteer seriously, then, is what adoptive ministry is all about.

Now the table is set and the meal is ready. It's time to roll up our sleeves and serve our young siblings.

PART THREE

The Fundamental Practices of Adoptive Churches

In this final stage of implementing adoptive youth ministry in churches, we get at the heart of what will create the kind of environment where young people can experience what it means to live as members of God's household. This final section looks at nurturing (chap. 9) and empowering (chap. 10) our young siblings. While over the years youth ministers have sought to do both of these, our attempts have generally been confined to the youth ministry setting. In this section we will explore and rethink our assumptions about programming and participation levels and our attitudes toward young people as we nurture them and their faith and empower them as siblings in the broader family of God.

The final chapter talks about change. Here we pull together what ministry to the young—what I have called "adoptive youth ministry"—can look like in a faith community where everyone is on board. Our final task is to convince the unconvinced to love, nurture, empower, and welcome children, adolescents, and emerging adults as siblings in the household of faith.

Adoptive youth ministry is, after all, not new. It is ultimately about Jesus Christ and his kingdom and the household God has given to us to serve and represent him in the world. Adoptive youth ministry is about our young, and our not so young, and the family that God is calling them to in Christ.

9

Nurture and the Ministry of Going

The three volunteers were right out of college. Having spent years studying youth ministry, they were now ready to plunge in and minister. After lunch, the four of us headed to the high school to spend time with students, also known as "contact work." The school's administration had given us permission to come onto the campus to see kids as long as we were not there to "proselytize." I promised the administration that was fine.

"OK, guys," I said as I parked the car. "Who wants to pray?"

"Why pray?" my friend Brandon asked.

As we talked, Brandon assured me he wasn't against praying. "I think it's important to pray before you teach or preach," he said. "And I think all the staff and volunteers should pray before a youth meeting. But I never really thought about praying before contact work."

A wonderful opportunity had presented itself, and I took advantage.

"Guys, Brandon raises a good point," I said. "But here's how I see this. *Every time* we go somewhere to see and serve students, I want to make sure we are seeing what Christ wants us to see and meeting who he wants us to meet. Praying before you teach is great, but praying before you go to meet students is important too. Let's pray that God will open our eyes, our ears, and our hearts as we go to the school."

One of the guys prayed, and then we walked into the school for a couple of intense hours of connecting. We talked to some of our regulars and also met some new friends.

Afterward, I asked Brandon what he thought.

"Awesome," he said. "I had this sense that God was helping me listen more to what the kids were saying instead of always thinking about something I wanted to say."

That day, Brandon experienced the nurturing side of adoptive youth ministry. All of us are familiar with the more public sides of ministry: teaching, preaching, and organizing events. But the quieter, subtler, more interpersonal connections between leaders and the students they serve can go a long way toward helping young people develop a relationship with Christ and with their siblings in the Christian community.

From What to Why

Today I saw this advertisement for a church seeking a youth leader:

> We are looking for an experienced director of student ministry to lead and expand ministry with seventh grade through twelfth grade students and leaders. Our youth ministry seeks to build community, grow through God's word, and reach area youth with the gospel of Jesus Christ. We have up to forty-five students in our weekly programs with around seventy registered as "active" in the church. Major responsibilities include Sunday morning Sunday school, evening youth groups, monthly events, discipleship groups, summer camps, and mission trips.

I have read hundreds of these youth leader ads, which typically focus on programmatic activities:

- Organize Sunday school
- Lead evening youth groups
- Devise monthly events
- Form discipleship groups
- Organize summer camps and mission trips

There's one common denominator in these bullet items: the assumption that youth ministry is what we *do* with the kids who come to us. The expectation is that youth leaders put on programs that are centered on the church building and church schedule. If we do these actions well, it is assumed the job's goals will be accomplished. That's the way things are at most churches.

For many churches and church people, this is the only way to do youth ministry: hire a leader to do activities and events. If we build the program, kids will come and their lives will be changed.

There's a problem with this model. It isn't working. Yes, many students may come, but how many of them eventually stop coming? And even if they stay in our program for a while, will they start a lifelong journey of following Jesus there?

Adoptive youth ministry is different. We are far less concerned with *what* we do and much more concerned with *why* we do it and how we are moving young people toward a connection with Christ and his family. Adoptive ministry leaders are fine with "evening youth groups" or other events on the church calendar. But they're not convinced that successfully organizing such events equals success with kids.

Let's examine one sacred cow: Sunday school. This might work fine for some youth ministries, but let's remember, Sunday school isn't ministry. Sunday school is a tool we use to achieve ministry. The same goes for events, discipleship groups, and trips. As good and productive as these and other programmatic elements can be, *they are not ministry but ways to express ministry.*

This subtle switch from *what* to *why* is key to the success of adoptive youth ministry. Programs and activities can be great tools, but these are not the only tools we need to help students journey from the often lonely, disconnected world of adolescence or emerging adulthood into the household of God and all that comes with it.

Programs and events do not define our ministry, and we must never let them confine our ministry or hinder us from our original goals. We can't rely on programs to move young people toward greater participation in God's family. We need to nurture them, which means showing the kind of care that helps them grow and develop.

Why Nurture Is about Going

We've been talking about *what* versus *why*. Let's add another *w* to the mix: *where*.

When leaders assume that their main job is to fulfill all the programmatic bullet items in the job description, they can forget a crucial command of Christ: to go. Instead of going to gather in lost sheep we can nurture, we take the opposite approach: "If we build it, they will come to us!" We expect the lost sheep to come to us.

Adoptive ministry embraces an intentional and proactive commitment to *going* in the direction of someone in need in order to nurture and care for them. That was my goal with Brandon and the other volunteers when we did contact work at the high school. I was emphasizing going, not teaching, preaching, or organizing events.

Why does adoptive ministry require us to go in order to nurture? There are four main reasons for this emphasis on going, and they are summed up in the following words: *mobile*, *familial*, *communal*, and *strategic*.

Nurture Is Mobile

If you ask some Christians what the incarnation is, they will tell you it's something related to Christmas celebrations. But for adoptive ministry leaders, incarnation means so much more than that.

Incarnation is the word we use to describe God's movement to our material world in the person of Jesus. "In the beginning was the Word, and the Word was with God, and the Word was God" (John 1:1). "The Word became flesh and blood, and moved into the neighborhood" (John 1:14 Message).

The incarnation sets the Christian faith apart from all others. While the incarnation was a one-time event, God was intentionally reaching into creation long before he sent his Son to earth. From the very beginning, God was a visiting God. He walked in the garden, looking for the hiding Adam and Eve (Gen. 3:8–9). God is a *going* God, a pursuing Lover. The incarnation isn't the beginning of this story but its fulfillment. During Jesus's life on earth, God continued to walk among us in new and amazing ways.

Jesus began his public ministry walking among the people and calling his disciples to follow him. Matthew tells us that "as Jesus was walking beside the Sea of Galilee, he saw two brothers, Simon called Peter and his brother Andrew." Watching them fish, Jesus said to them, "Come, follow me, and I will send you out to fish for people" (Matt. 4:18–19).

One day Jesus was traveling through the land of the despised Samaritan people (John 4:4 says he "had to go through Samaria"). He sat down at a deserted well outside of town; he had sent the disciples into town to buy food. Soon a woman approached the well and, although it was outside both religious and social rules, Jesus initiated a conversation with her that would transform her life, as she became the first evangelist in the Gospel of John to a town where she was an outcast! It is as if Jesus had decided to put himself in the position to be there when she showed up (again, "he had to go through Samaria"—*nobody* has "to go through Samaria"; there were other options). The way the connection unfolded—Jesus sending his disciples off without him, sitting alone by a well, waiting, and then honoring a woman with a tough history by speaking to her, affirming her value by taking the dialogue to pretty deep places, and finally openly telling her that he was the expected Savior—indicates that this is no ordinary encounter. He was there, with her and for her, and his initiative altered her story in a way that changed her and her town's life. Jesus *had* to go through Samaria.

Jesus never stayed put. He constantly traveled, observed, listened, and cared. His ministry of nurture was a going, mobile ministry. Likewise, Jesus sent his disciples to go and minister in his name. He told them in Luke 9:2 "to proclaim the kingdom of God and to heal the sick." He goes further in Luke 10:1. He "appointed seventy-two others and sent them two by two ahead of him to every town and place where he was about to go." And in the upper room with his disciples after the resurrection, Jesus told them, "As the Father has sent me, I am sending you" (John 20:21).

After Jesus had ascended into heaven (Acts 1:9), the disciples gathered together to pray and wait for the Holy Spirit to direct their next steps. The Spirit arrived in power on the day of Pentecost. Jews from many nations who had gathered in Jerusalem for the holy day were shocked to hear Jesus's message spoken in their own languages by the power of the Spirit. This was the early church's first big evangelistic event, and it added thousands to the embryonic household of God (Acts 2).

Later, as the church was scattered because of persecution, leaders like Philip heeded Jesus's call to take the good news to the "ends of the earth" (Acts 1:8). Later still, Paul took three major trips in order to come alongside others to minister to those who needed the love and grace of the Savior. In his first letter to the Thessalonians, Paul reminds them that his and his companion's "visit to [them] was not without results" (1 Thess. 2:1).

The early church knew that ministry means going to those who are in need of the gospel and of the love of Christ's body. Somewhere along the line we seem to have forgotten this. Adoptive ministry is mobile. It seeks to resurrect this lost calling, particularly in church-centered youth ministry.

You will search the New Testament in vain for any hint of our contemporary "build it and they will come" methodology. Christ was a man on the move, and Christians were a faith community committed to going.

Nurture Is Familial

As early disciples went, they took their brothers and sisters in the Christian family with them. Paul shows that ministry should be as nurturing as a mother's love: "We were gentle among you.[1] Just as a nursing mother cares for her children, so we cared for you. Because we loved you so much, we were delighted to share with you not only the gospel of God but our lives as well" (1 Thess. 2:7–8).

Look carefully and you can see Paul addressing four aspects of nurture:

1. Nurture is *gentle*. We do all we can to avoid being harsh, or shaming, in our nurture of a student's faith and life.
2. Nurture is *caring* and *loving*. Our commitment in nurturing a young person is to reflect the kindness and tenderness of a maternal touch.
3. Nurture involves sharing *the gospel of God*. We don't do that by hammering away at kids with a barrage of empty argumentation. Instead, we simply share the good news of our adoption into God's family by his mercy and grace.
4. Nurture involves sharing *your own life experience* with the people you care for. Paul reminded the Thessalonians of his trials and tribulations on their behalf. He shared his life with them. (Note: this is not an endorsement of the kind of no-holds-barred social media sharing that lands so many people in trouble.)

Nurture Is Communal

What's the best way to disciple a young person? When I raise that question, many people express support for the one-on-one mentoring model. I know many believers who swear by this approach, which involves one mature believer guiding one who is younger in the faith.

I have mentored younger believers, and older leaders have mentored me. It's a solid model. But adoptive ministry proposes an important tweak.

We believe the ministry of nurture is best delivered in community. God's household is not a collection of isolated mentors and mentees, but a family of co-mentoring siblings. In God's big family, we love all our siblings, and we naturally nurture one another, keeping no record or score of who is nurturing the other person most. It's not a contest. We all share in the familial call to care for our brothers and sisters in Christ.

Familial nurturing is exactly what so many kids today want and need. As we grow into our adoption in God's family, and grow in our love of each other, this nurturing atmosphere becomes a powerful way to draw kids into full participation in the household of God. All of us have been knit together through adoption, and all of us—adults and students—nurture one another in community.

Nurture Is Strategic

Nurture may sound warm and fuzzy, but it's also strategic. Adoptive youth ministry wants to create the kind of welcoming space where young people can explore the message of the gospel and move incrementally into deeper faith. Programs alone can't create that kind of space. We need to do what Jesus did to create an environment where trust and transformation take place.

Jesus went to the woman at the well. She would not have initiated the conversation herself. He reached out to her at a shared space: a well. (Today he might visit high schools, libraries, or coffee shops.) In that space she could feel his warmth. That's all she needed to trust him. The setting was safe, and they talked. When he told her he was "the one," she immediately ran to tell the world, "Come, see a man who told me everything I ever did. Could this be the Messiah?" (John 4:29).

Adoptive nurture is strategic. It creates spaces where we tell kids: You matter to us. We care about you. We're not asking you to sign on a dotted line. We just want to share some of our family's love with you. Or as J. B. Phillips translates it, "Because we loved you, it was a joy to us to give you not only the Gospel of God but our very hearts—so dear did you become to us" (1 Thess. 2:8).

From *Why* Back to *What*: Gathering Together

Some people get so caught up in the *what* of ministry that they forget the *why*. Now that we've explored why we must go and why we must nurture, let's go back to the what of activities and programs.

We need to do activities and events with kids. We can organize these activities so they achieve the goals of adoptive youth ministry if we keep our focus on our three main reasons for gathering: to build trust, to build warmth, and to explore Christ's good news together.

We Gather to Build Trust

When we get together, we have fun. We play (even though some killjoys claim play and fun have no place in adolescent ministry).[2] We enjoy games together that you can't enjoy sitting alone in a room with a phone or laptop.

Why? Getting young people to smile is often the first step toward helping them feel safe. Even on an otherwise serious mission trip or leadership retreat, there's nothing better than for everyone to jump in a lake with their clothes on, or run around spraying the leader with Silly String. One of the greatest gifts adolescents bring to a faith community is that they still know how to have a blast.

Smiles help build trust. When we are flying down a zip line, or having a mud fight, or watching an obnoxiously flippant but oh-so-funny video, students have the ability to say, "These people actually want me to have fun! It's not all about them; they know I need to let loose sometimes!" As we play together, we find ourselves more open to sharing the deeper issues of our lives together. And this is essential to helping kids prepare for inclusion within God's household of siblings.

We Gather to Build Warmth

A warm community is what every young person seeks. A place of safety. A place where they can let down, take off their shoes, and sip hot cocoa with their closest friends in the midst of a cold winter storm.

Many researchers have discovered that for collaboration to be genuine and heartfelt, people need to feel the warmth of the community. In the study detailed in *Growing Young*, Powell, Mulder, and Griffin note that "we were surprised by how much of growing young is influenced by whether or not congregations are warm and accepting."[3] Adoptive nurture, then, is creating the space that every young person feels is warm and accepting when we gather.

As Paul shows, ministry means sharing "not only the gospel of God but our lives as well" (1 Thess. 2:8). Adoptive nurture takes place within a gathering of young people where friendship and safety are the highest values. Conformity and competition are out; unity and acceptance are in.

To nurture the young, we need to value laughter over lectures, and authentic connection over Christian acculturation. There is ample time in a warm, nurturing, familial atmosphere to dissect and examine what real-life faith is, means, and looks like. But it is vital that our adoptive nurture is located within a gathering that can only be described as warm.

We Gather to Explore Christ's Good News Together

Why do we sing at our gatherings? Why do we teach? When I attend youth ministry gatherings, events, camps, and retreats, I often head to the back of the room during the singing and teaching times. I want to experience what the whole group is experiencing. Up front, the sophomore girls are waving their hands and praising God, but things feel totally different in the back half of the room.

That's where most of the guys and many of the girls are sitting (unless the leader compels them to stand). Sometimes it seems they're checked out. They might be talking to each other, or staring into space, or even trying to sort of sing without being totally into it.

Why the poor response? It's not because they do not long to worship God, at least not all of them. Rather, for many, what we call "worship" seems like people screaming over a cheesy performance by a band of rock-and-roll wannabes.

Why do we sing at our gatherings? Why do we teach? We say we are presenting the gospel in a relevant way that connects to young people's lives. That's not the way it always looks from the back half of the room.

Let's sing with gusto. Let's teach the truth with passion. But let's do these things in a way that brings us together as God's family. Instead of relying on a group of elite performers, let's create spaces and gatherings that build trust and facilitate warmth among the entire group.

We need to find ways to nurture *every* student, not just the ones who might love group singing or solo teaching. Our task in adoptive nurture is to know our students well enough to maintain the trust and warmth we work so hard to cultivate. Then when the time comes to explore the gospel, that exploration will be okay because it is nestled within that familial relational setting.

You may need to let kids talk to you as you teach. You will survive.

Better yet, find ways for them to share things that matter to them with the group: a meaningful poem, a funny video clip, a sad text message from a friend, or a Bible verse that encourages them.

Let's sing. Let's study Scripture together. But let's also use other tools that help us create the spaces where safe, warm, communal relationships can flourish.

10

Beyond Participation

THE POWER OF EMPOWERMENT

Educational experts say about 6 percent of American children meet this definition for "gifted and talented": "Students, children, or youth who give evidence of high achievement capability in areas such as intellectual, creative, artistic, or leadership capacity, or in specific academic fields, and who need services and activities not ordinarily provided by the school in order to fully develop those capabilities."[1] So what about the remaining 94 percent? Don't they have gifts and talents? And where did this "gifted and talented" lingo come from, anyway?

In 1954 the National Association of Gifted Children was founded on the premise that some children are gifted in ways that most children are not. The concept was given official status with the creation of the US Department of Education's Office of the Gifted and Talented in 1974.[2] In time the concept percolated through education circles and American culture.

Decades later, our kids are growing up in a world that pretty much embraces the concept that there are very few top-performing students and then there's everybody else. Many young people I've known feel certain they're in the vast 94 percent, not the elite 6 percent. It is a heavy burden on kids' shoulders to go through life believing that experts have already determined they don't have "it," whatever "it" is. And that applies to those we love to call "normal" kids. What does this say about the 6.7 million young people in the US who are classified as needing "special education services"?[3] Do these not represent another subset of those who are deserving of not only our nurture and welcome but also an intentional commitment from us to empower each one to bring their unique gifts and love to the body of Christ? My friend Miri Sampson, who works with Capernaum Ministries, a branch of Young Life, recently reminded me of the power and profound grace that each of these all-too-often forgotten kids and their families offer to everyone they encounter. When we buy in to how the world only sees the superstar—the athlete, the singer, the "beautiful"—we miss out on that subtle but overwhelming blessing that God gives us through those we deem invisible.

That's why it breaks my heart when I see church and youth ministries unwittingly slip into this "gifted and talented" mindset. We might not use that lingo, but we make the same kinds of distinctions among our kids, treating our "best" students differently than we treat the others. You may not see it, but your students can.

You may call your approach "student leadership." You may encourage "those God has blessed with the gift of music" to sing a song for the community. Some kids are blessed and can speak or play guitar. Meanwhile, the other kids wonder, "Why hasn't God blessed me with any talents?"

One prominent Christian high school in Southern California devoted a special student assembly to one star football player. Faculty and administration didn't see any problem with the celebration, but one local youth pastor asked a pointed question: "When will we have a special student assembly for the students who build the sets for the school play? Or the students who tutor urban kids?"

"When they get a scholarship to Notre Dame, that's when!" said one administrator.

Many youth ministries have mindlessly baptized the concept of gifted and talented. We've also added on a dangerous theological component by insinuating that gifted and talented kids are uniquely blessed by God. Everybody else? Not blessed quite so much.

Adoptive churches expose this concept for what it is: a heresy that denies the varied gifts and talents God graciously bestows on each and every one of us, regardless of merit or social status. In an adoptive church, we not only recognize that everyone in our group is blessed and gifted; we put that belief into practice by intentionally involving everyone in the life of the community.

Isn't that what siblings do in their families?

This is the power of empowerment. Let's see how we can empower everyone in our communities to use and develop their gifts within the loving embrace of God's big family.

The Journey of Empowerment: Everyone Participating and Contributing

Adult leaders say they want *all* kids to participate, but what do they mean? Participation means different things to different groups. Most kids realize that some form of participation is the price they must pay to be part of a group. But what's the fun of being a member of the team if you never get to play in a real game? Minimalist participation is only minimally effective!

Some groups actively encourage kids to participate, but only so far. Kids can help in the sound booth as long as they don't turn up the drums too loud. They can "teach" second-grade Sunday school if they follow the curriculum to the letter. Many adults believe the best way to help kids realize they are part of the church family is to give them only small, token assignments.

Our students are growing up in a culture where some groups award "participation trophies" to any living and breathing kids who show up. Millennial-bashers love talking about these trophies, blaming this generation's "entitlement" woes on receiving empty prizes. "These kids only participated. Why do they think they deserve a trophy?"

Adoptive youth ministry seeks more than minimal participation. We want young people to experience what it's like to live as a part of the family of God. Our hope is that they grow in that family and increasingly contribute their God-given gifts and talents for the building up of the whole family.

But many kids may not feel equipped to contribute anything of worth to the family. They've been taught they're part of the nongifted and nontalented masses, and they believe it. That's why we must empower them.

Inviting only kids' participation without offering any real empowerment is an empty gesture. But things change when we believe deep down that middle school students do have something of substance to offer, and then we help them offer it.

Would your church trust a trained and qualified twenty-three-year-old college student to chair the missions department and oversee its budget of thousands of dollars from members' tithes? Could we give voice to a high school student who was willing to be taught and study the Scriptures and as a result felt called to offer critique and advice for a pastor's sermon series? Behind these nagging questions lies one much larger and more troubling question: *Do we really trust our teenage and young adult siblings to contribute alongside us now, even if they are willing and trained, or must they wait until we finally deem them ready to serve God's family?*

Power to the People: Four Keys to Empowering Our Younger Siblings

It's one thing to talk about empowering young people and another to make it happen. Sometimes it's not a question of whether students have the ability to serve, but a question of power. Adults have the power, and some don't want to share it with "those kids." Empowerment is a major theological issue for some adults. For others it's a major psychosocial issue.

We need to transcend participation and go all out for contribution. A participant is *allowed* to be with us. A contributor is a coworker we must listen to and take seriously.

I was a principal researcher for the Fuller Youth Institute's Churches Engaging Young People (CEYP) project. We looked at which groups preferred participation and which preferred contribution. On the surface these perspectives can look pretty much the same. But look beneath the surface and you can see the difference in the way young people feel about their relationship to the group depending on how included they feel. The authors of *Growing Young*, the book describing this research, repeatedly noted in their background work (called a literature review) the difference between being a participant and being a contributor.[4] Groups that empower the young to contribute can experience two related benefits:

- Empowering groups discover a wealth of untapped resources they previously overlooked.
- Empowering groups are actually the best way to develop long-term coworkers and ministry partners.

Adoptive empowerment wants to make sure that when the church, the organization, or the youth group receives young people as siblings, they commit to receiving their contributions to the family. Yes, younger partners may need some level of training and apprenticeship for some forms of ministry. But there's no training required for them to bring a fresh perspective to any community.

Empowerment is our goal. We want teenagers and emerging adults to be embraced not only as younger siblings but also as valued ministry partners. To reach this goal we need to recognize four keys to empowering the young, summed up in these four words: *intergenerational*, *particular*, *incremental*, and *intentional*.

Empowerment Is Intergenerational

I assume most readers already know that to be effective, youth ministry should be intergenerational, but putting that into practice is not always easy. Throwing five senior adults and five ninth graders in a van for an ill-conceived service project doesn't automatically produce lifelong friendships. A slapdash approach may actually make it harder to build intergenerational bridges.

Seniors don't always know how to talk to kids, and kids aren't sure how to approach seniors. There may be an outlier or two who are able to break through the generational and cultural barriers. More often it seems students don't see the need for reaching out, and some of the adults don't either.

Holly Catterton Allen, a child and family studies professor, says that within intergenerational congregations all age groups "grow each other up into Christ."[5] Every fifteen-year-old needs older siblings in order to grow in Christ and experience a long-term faith. Likewise, every sixty-five-year-old needs a fifteen-year-old sibling to keep things real!

We need each other. If you want that to be the reality in your community, the adults must commit to embracing the following attitudes and actions:

- They see their role as initiators of relationship, so they don't wait for young people to take the lead in building community.
- They are trained to recognize and understand key stages of adolescent development and emerging adulthood so that they can help young people navigate these changes.
- They can identify their own subjective biases and attitudes so that they can avoid behaviors that weaken community, such as shaming, labeling, and lecturing.
- They inundate young people with words and actions that demonstrate they are loved, valued, and respected.

Churches that want to create a community where every voice is heard and every person is valued need to foster the kind of environment where intergenerational relationships flourish.

Empowerment Is Particular

Some people love humanity but hate individual people. Likewise, many churches say they value young people, but few actually open up church power structures to young people's contributions.

Empowering an individual does not happen without a carefully designed and executed ministry plan that makes including each student the end goal of ministry. As I've said throughout this book, the goal of adoptive youth ministry is to create an environment where young people are encouraged to live into their calling in Christ as agents of the kingdom within the household of God.

To achieve that goal, we need to drop macro-platitudes, roll up our sleeves, and create a micro-growth plan for each individual young person at every stage in their ministry journey. Adoptive empowerment isn't some kind of pixie dust we sprinkle on a group of kids. It requires a laser-like focus on welcoming, including, nurturing, and repeatedly empowering youth to contribute to this community in a way that will enhance the body while encouraging their growth.

Adoptive ministry may use the traditional tools of youth ministry (youth groups, small groups), but the long-term goal is creating a plan to lead young people toward ever-greater levels of maturity and contribution within God's family.

Empowerment Is Incremental

Wouldn't it be easy if everyone was the same and grew at the same rate? Such assumptions have supported massive public education programs that impose standardized learning outcomes on all the different age groups of kids.

Such standardized outcomes weren't ideal for me. If you could go back to the time when I was a gangly sixteen-year-old and ask my parents, my siblings, or my high school friends where they thought I would end up in life, none would have predicted graduate school professor. I wasn't much of a student. I only ended up at Fuller Seminary as a master's student in theology because of my passion to be on Young Life staff. Young Life made me go to Fuller (like they did all their staff for over three decades).

Who knew I would end up not only loving theological study but also loving to pass that passion on to others? Before that, my road was a winding, up-and-down journey for the first twenty-five years of my life.

That's the case for many young people in today's disrupted economy. The activities they're interested in and good at as teenagers may have little to do with what they end up devoting their lives to. Along the way we all go through fits and starts, detours and U-turns. Growth is incremental.

While schools impose standardized learning outcomes, churches often do something similar by trying to fit people into a series of standardized measures of spiritual growth. But often spiritual growth occurs in baby steps that can't be measured. Chuck Swindoll understood this, titling his classic book on discipleship *Three Steps Forward, Two Steps Back*.

To empower our young to contribute to the community of siblings, we need to allow them and assist them to move at their own pace. The *Growing Young* authors describe this as "keychain leadership."[6]

Adoptive empowerment does not mean handing over the keys to someone who doesn't know what keys are, or what they unlock. We don't simply hand keys to young people and walk away. We walk alongside them as they take baby steps, grow, and learn how to use keys. Empowerment means we assume a high view of each person's abilities and giftedness in Christ and help create baby steps that allow them to move toward greater maturity.

For example, if a sophomore in high school, or even an eighth grader, shows interest and promise in what missions can do for people in your congregation, an appropriate baby step could be inviting her to observe the planning team for a trip she would probably be interested in joining. Just by being invited to sit at the table, she has been affirmed and shown that her presence matters.

Granted, this may look like participation rather than contribution, but it is a start. As the meetings progress, adults (or the whole team) who are watching out for her growth and journey may see a unique piece of the planning process where she shows interest or insight. At that point, the student could be invited to *join* an adult or small subgroup in working on that planning.

In some cases, young people who are given such opportunities rise to the occasion and demonstrate unusual maturity. In other cases, they flake out or disappear. This is consistent with the nature of adolescents in transition, so you need to prepare adults for the occasional flameout. But don't let these defections lead adults to conclude that all kids lack interest or maturity. Adults need to be the grown-ups, continuing to offer relational support and stability. At the same time, accountability should always be practiced in a nurturing and encouraging environment. Don't let the "two steps back" stop your church or team from continuing to both believe in and move toward empowering each and every young person.

Empowerment Is Intentional

The final point to make is that adults must take responsibility to be the driving initiators of relationship and interaction. This is one of those realities that few adults get, and even the ones who get it don't like it!

When students or emerging adults believe that adults perceive them as unreliable or disengaged, surprisingly many will default by living more deeply into that negative perception. Young people may hate being stereotyped, but their attitudes and behavior can easily fulfill the stereotypes. In this way, young people become their own worst enemies, frustrating efforts toward greater participation and contribution.

But there is more to the story. Nearly all young people desperately *want* to be part of something bigger than themselves, and their intent is to be seen as valuable and committed. Adults who work with adolescents and young adults have to be trained to recognize this vocational paradox, and not to be deterred by it.

Making Empowerment Intentional

If empowerment happened naturally, everyone would be empowered! But it doesn't, and we often need to believe the best about young people, even when their behavior may not affirm or support it.

That's why leaders committed to helping empower students need to be intentional in three ways: communication, affirmation, and support.

Intentional Communication

An important marker of maturity is to communicate well with others. When we're walking with those who are in developmental transition, we are the ones who need to keep lines of communication open.

Early in my ministry I was taught the value of "short accounts" and timely engagement. This means that when I'm leading a group and I become disappointed or confused about the way a student has behaved, it is up to me to move as swiftly as possible to find out what is going on and why.

In the meantime, while we're working at the intersection of nurturing young people and empowering them, we must work to ensure that our questions and style of communication are not confrontational or shaming. This is a learned skill that, frankly, many adults have not learned or practiced, so leaders must train the team. This correcting and training is best done face-to-face, or with rare exceptions, on the phone. Email and texting are the worst modes for communicating a perceived failure or misunderstanding. The key is to maintain a relational closeness to a young person so that even when they fail or flake out, they know that their leader/mentor is consistent and trustworthy enough that they can be open and honest about their misstep.

Intentional Affirmation

Ministry is important, but people matter more than any task. This is one of those affective aspects of guiding and mentoring that is essential in helping a young person mature to the point of contribution. If a seventeen-year-old knows that he is more important than the duty to pick up the coffee for the parent meeting, he can survive setbacks and continue on with his growth and service.

Intentional Support

Sometimes young people simply need time and space away from ministry or even church for a while. This can be due to a variety of circumstances, and how we handle their distance from church-related things will often determine how or whether the student will reengage in the future.

Our job is to seek the very best for all students, communicate well, and make sure they know that our support for them is absolute. Sometimes that means trying to help them work through the timing and consequences of stepping away from something they agreed to do. Hopefully, we can help them find a way to get the time and space they need without hurting others. Our attitude and spirit in such cases can make all the difference in their long-term growth.

I learned about a relevant case study at a recent pastors' conference. One pastor lamented an experience that still clearly bugged him. He had "allowed" (his word) a young college student to run a Saturday service project. A week before the event the young man bailed on him via text: "I am so overwhelmed, I just can't do it. I'm sure you'll find someone else to take it, but I will not be at the service project." The pastor tried to "hold him accountable" via text, and he let the young man know how "disappointed" he was in his choice.

I invited the gathered pastors to respond, making suggestions about what the pastor could have done differently. For example, the pastor could have met face-to-face with the young person within hours of the first text. That would have reflected both pastoral concern and programmatic integrity. Others wondered if the pastor had developed a meaningful relationship with the student before this episode.

It's obvious that we don't want to encourage irresponsibility when we invite young people to contribute. But we need to be careful how we respond to them when they fail to perform as we wish. Our aim must be to offer young people support.

Making Empowerment Practical: Creating a Youth Advisory Board

Too many leaders still think the goal is participation. But participation is weak when compared with true contribution. If your ministry practices adoptive empowerment, odds are your group will be full of young people who go to bed at night thinking, "I made a difference today, and I was an important part of my church family. Thanks, Jesus!"

There are as many ways to empower young people to contribute as there are churches. But the various approaches have one thing in common. When we offer opportunities with intention, warmth, and consistent nurturing presence, young people will feel like they matter to the family of God.

In closing this chapter, I want to offer one concrete step a church can take. It's simple, straightforward, and requires no programming. All that's needed is a bit of courage, some initiative, and leadership consistency to encourage young people to rise to the occasion.

Here's my suggestion: create an advisory board for the preaching ministry of the church made up entirely of young people.

Let's face it. Few high school students or recent grads deeply resonate with the sermons they hear on Sundays. But the Fuller Youth Institute's College Transition Project found that of those young people who held on to faith, a major factor they cited was that they "liked church" when they were in high school.

That's why I believe every church should invite sixteen- to twenty-year-olds to be a part of a group that helps the preaching pastor or teaching team engage them and hear their concerns. A church can invite a few kids to do this, or enlist a much larger contingent. The number of students doesn't matter so long as they are willing to do four things:

1. Attend church every week, as much as is possible, for an entire season or sermon series.
2. Take detailed and extensive notes on everything from the opening lines to illustrations to the study of the biblical text.
3. Take some time to reflect on every aspect of the sermon, including looking up Scriptures used, consulting commentaries, asking others' opinions, and keeping a journal of their perspective.
4. Attend a meeting with the pastor (or pastors) to share their thoughts.

When I mention this to pastors, some balk, many are nervous, but most are so grateful to have the chance to get to know their students at this level.

I am honest. I tell pastors that if they are really open, young people may occasionally be brutally honest, and even sometimes unfair. But in a very short time, they will grow into a greater appreciation of the role of preaching and teaching in a church. The added benefit? These kids will not only know that their voices are being heard and they are being taken seriously, but they will also likely end up being among the best friends a senior pastor has ever had in a congregant.

Adoptive youth ministry must find ways not only to nurture the young but to intentionally, proactively, and enthusiastically encourage and empower them to contribute to the mission of God. The word *empower* means "to impart power." That requires someone who has power to hand off that power. Empowerment is what helps an adolescent build a sense of self and healthy autonomy. Empowerment also encourages a sense of purpose, a necessary aspect to interdependent adulthood. And the most important reason we empower our young to participate and contribute? We need them!

11

Adoptive Youth Ministry and the Challenge of Change

Fundamentally, Christ intends that the pastoral office facilitate the spiritual growth of the community so that all can engage in the common task (Eph. 4:12). To this end, pastors keep up for the people the vision of community life embodied in the biblical narrative.

—Stanley Grenz, *Created for Community*[1]

When I talk to youth workers and churches about embracing adoptive youth ministry, most seem excited, at least initially. Then come the doubts and reservations.

"Chap," they say, "you just don't know what I'm dealing with." Then follows a litany of complaints about elders, deacons, boards or sessions, parents, older church members, or occasionally the senior pastor.

"We don't have any power to change things or embrace a new approach without starting World War III," they say, signaling defeat and sometimes despair.

But you don't need to overhaul your entire congregation in order to integrate adoptive youth ministry into your work with young people. As Fuller Seminary leadership professor Scott Cormode has shown, even youth workers who are relatively low on the ecclesiastical organizational chart can play an important part in bringing about transformation. "Christian leadership is fundamentally an act of theological interpretation," writes Cormode. "A Christian leader today leads by shaping the ways that God's people interpret everything going on in their worlds."[2]

Do you ever think of yourself as a theologian or a theological interpreter? You may not, but in fact you are! Youth workers not only interpret Scripture to their students, but they also help adults in the church understand how the truths of Scripture connect with young believers.

You can help shape the way that God's people understand young people and their spiritual needs. To do that, you first need to understand why so many people have so many problems with change of any kind.

Confronting the Challenge of Change

Why are so many people so resistant to change? Scott Cormode says the proposed changes themselves are not the whole problem. "People don't resist change, they resist loss," he writes, "and to understand longing and loss is to understand how people are not only wired but how they can change."[3]

Even when we want the new things change brings, we struggle to resist the stranglehold that old things have us in. Sure, millions of us appreciate Amazon's discounts and algorithms when it means we can buy a new book for less money. But at the same time, we miss the old bookstore we used to go to and the helpful workers there who always managed to make personal recommendations that we loved.

We tend to fear losing those things we have relied on in the past to bring order, meaning, and comfort to our lives. Our longings for meaning and order often drive our fear, resentment, and need for control. And these powerful longings sometimes play an even stronger role in church settings, where proposals to change *anything* will be interpreted by some as a declaration of ecclesial war. (Ask me sometime and I will show you my battle scars!)

There are four main reasons change can be a bigger challenge for church folks than for others. The better you understand these reasons, the better you can address them.

Volunteers and Donors Who Feel They "Own" the Church

Most churches are volunteer-run and volunteer-supported organizations that depend on people choosing to stay involved. This means those who devote the time and those who write the checks tend to accumulate power. That power can express itself in emotive ways when someone like you comes along and threatens to upset the applecart.

It's understandable that believers who have devoted years of their lives and many thousands of their dollars to support the congregation will seek to protect it from harm. Unfortunately, they often see change as harmful, even when it's desperately needed.

Their position is clear, even though they may not always state it this boldly: "This is our church. We built it and we paid for it. Don't you dare mess with it!"

The Four Main Reasons Change Can Be a Bigger Challenge for Church Folks

1. Volunteers and donors who feel they "own" the church
2. Members who want the church to honor their longings
3. Bondage to history
4. It takes work!

I was helping a church develop a strategic plan when a fight broke out over one of the words I used. It wasn't a swear word, or a heretical word, but a cultural word: video. The offending word was in a report I handed out.

"For years I have put my hard-earned money into this church, and nobody is going to come along and put up screens in my sanctuary!" one elder hollered during a discussion about how the church was dying and needed to reach younger people.

What had I done to incite such possessiveness and anger? I must have evoked some powerful fear of a world out of control. For better or worse, technology has upended our world in unsettling ways. This elder didn't want to unleash this chaotic force in "his" comfortable sanctuary.

"You raise an important question," I said. "Whose church is it, anyway?"

Key volunteers and donors deserve respect and praise, but they don't "own" the church. Christ does.

Members Who Want the Church to Honor Their Longings

Some people invest their time and treasure in churches out of a sense of service or calling. Other people connect with churches because they need the warm feelings it gives them. They want "to belong, find a place to share one's gifts, and be valued,"[4] writes Christine Pohl, professor of Christian social ethics at Asbury Seminary.

Churches are challenging environments for change because people go to church so they can satisfy their deep human longings for community and connection. This may mean they feel "closer to God" when they hear handbells, but don't you dare play a guitar. Even though it has been over half a century since Larry Norman first strummed his six-string, the worship wars over music styles continue in many congregations. Why? Because people come to church hoping to relieve their fears and struggles from the outside world. Many members may be considered "part of the community," but in their minds they may feel more connection to a tight-knit, like-minded subgroup that shares their perspectives and values. They feel safe within the relational walls of "their" church, which is the one place that shouldn't challenge or interfere with their longings.

One important note here: Young people are not the only ones who often feel like outsiders in a congregation. Senior adults, single and divorced people, ethnic minorities, people with disabilities, even those who do not live in the neighborhood may feel like the church is being taken or kept from them. Adoptive ministry is the call to include *any* people who feel displaced or disenfranchised. This adds an additional challenge to adoptive youth ministry. It is not just young people who deserve our nurture, empowerment, and inclusion. It is everybody.

Bondage to History

Institutions are shaped by their history. Therefore, history—including everything from informal use of power to programmatic structure and style of operation, and everything that goes on in making a given church community unique to itself—is a powerful force to be reckoned with. Harvard's Robert Putnam explains, "Whatever other factors may affect their form, institutions have inertia and 'robustness.' They therefore embody historical trajectories and turning points. History matters because it is 'path dependent': what comes first (even if it was in some sense 'accidental') conditions what comes later. Individuals may 'choose' their institutions, but they do not choose them under circumstances of their own making, and their choices in turn influence the rules within which their successors choose."[5]

Tradition is important, but you can tell history plays a crippling role in a congregation if you regularly hear comments like these:

- "We tried that once and it failed miserably."
- "That's not how we do it *here*."

The first uses history to discount new thinking or approaches. The second appeals to a church's supposed corporate narrative to close discussion on any approach that hasn't already been confirmed. Either way, the goal is to stop any change that threatens the community's historical narrative.

It Takes Work!

Churches are, after all, volunteer organizations. Typically, volunteer organizations try to fulfill their calling by doing what needs to be done when it needs to be done—then they want to be done with it! Phrases like "We've *always* done it this way" are not only indicators of fear of losing what people hold dear but also express a fear of changing what we already have figured out and know. To change is to wrestle, to explore, to risk. And this takes work: emotional work, physical work, and even spiritual work. Most people come to church to receive comfort and solace, not to be challenged to roll up their sleeves.

But the world has changed. And in many ways, for many of us, the church has not—at least not in the ways that matter, such as theologically and strategically. Ministries and programs traditionally have been fostered by creative, energetic people who genuinely care. But over time these programs control who we are and how we operate, *even if they do not actually help us to achieve our calling to become God's adoptive household!* In a changing context, with generations being increasingly marginalized and ignored, the church must change. If we intend to even somewhat reflect the kind of family that the Bible describes, we have no choice but to reflect more carefully on what it means for us to be and live into our calling as God's children together.

As an old illustration reminds us, laying bricks takes work, but building a cathedral takes calling. Creating an adoptive church, where every disconnected and marginalized person has the opportunity to be embraced, nurtured, and empowered by those at the center, is our charge. Yes, it takes time and conversation and careful biblical reflection. It also, then, takes baby steps to retool strategies and programs that align with our calling. Yet it is our privilege, and ultimately our joy, when we find ourselves growing more closely together, with greater appreciation for and understanding of one another. In the long run the work of ministry is not work at all; it is a life-giving gift of God when we allow ourselves to be careful and supportive of all members of our family.

Being an Effective Change Agent (Even When You're Not in Charge)

Reader, do not despair! While opposition to change is common, each congregation seems to have a few brave souls who believe new wine calls for new wineskins.

I just showed you how efforts to change things can backfire in some churches. Now let me show you how change can work effectively to bring new life to churches that struggle. Let me show what it might look like to bring change to any congregation, community, or organization in a healthy and theologically sound way.

If you were the chieftain of your own corporate kingdom, you could hire and fire at will. Things are different in Christ's body. For one thing, all members are created in the image of God and deserve your kindness and empathy, including those who are most resistant to change.

In dealing with hard-core obstructionists, the goal is not to force, coerce, or manipulate. The church belongs to God and God alone, and the veterans are siblings as much as the newcomers are. Adoptive ministry is about the family of Christ, so let's make sure everything we do is consistent with the kind of committed and selfless love Christ exhibited.

There are two basic ways to change any social system or structure. The most common—and often most painful—is mechanical or *technical change*, meaning you bring in an expert to "fix" a problem (like you find a mechanic when your car is broken).

That works for some challenges, but other, more complex problems require *adaptive change*.[6] As Scott Cormode puts it, "Adaptive challenges happen when we ask people to adopt new beliefs, when

Four Healthy Ways to Promote Change

1. Seek leadership buy-in, both theologically and programmatically.
2. Create a shared lexicon of words and phrases that reinforce community around key concepts.
3. Share narratives of adoptive youth ministry.
4. Experiment on the edges.

we hope people will pursue better values, or when we help people see that the ways that they have been doing things in the past will not work for them. Well, that's the job description for ministry."[7]

I have found four approaches that promote change in healthy ways. Let's take a look.

Seek Leadership Buy-In

I was sitting in on one church's tense monthly staff scheduling meeting when the pastor saw me involuntarily raise my eyebrows.

"Yes, Chap?" he asked.

"I was wondering if it had occurred to anyone what the connection was between Philippians 2:1–4 and the conversation at hand?"

Most of the staff knew their Bibles enough to know the text discussed unity. One person decided to read the passage. Then they looked back to me for interpretation.

"What would it mean for you all if each department decided to fight for the interests of another department?" I asked.

The mood changed as one person after another offered compromise that allowed the task at hand to be finished within minutes.

There are many ways to bring senior leadership into the adoptive conversation. The place to begin is with the theological question of who *we* are as the body of Christ, not what youth ministry needs to do or how to get senior adults and kids to like each other. Our starting point is God's intent for all of us.

After all, John 1:12 and Paul's use of "adoption to sonship" five times (Rom. 8:15, 23; 9:4; Gal. 4:5; Eph. 1:5) become crystal clear once someone sees it. It is impossible to discount the importance of Jesus's words in John 15, especially verses 1–17: "I am the vine; you [all] are the branches. . . . Apart from me you can do nothing. . . . My command is this: Love each other."

The only thing really new about adoptive youth ministry is the phrase "adoptive youth ministry"! The basic theological premise of adoptive ministry is thoroughly biblical and ultimately straight-forward. The challenge is reenvisioning everything we do and are in the direction of what God has called us to be. That is adoptive ministry.

As staff and lay leaders in your congregation warm up to the goal of God's people working out their life together in community so as to be fully prepared and free to participate in the mission of God in the world, the next step in designing an adoptive youth ministry is inviting a congregation or community to simply live into that truth with kids. This book encourages those in positions of power to invite, include, nurture, and empower those on the fringes to join them in God's mission, internally and externally—this is at the core of the adoptive ministry model. Again, the first step of making adoptive youth ministry a reality is to convince congregational leadership that youth ministry, and ultimately every ministry, is grounded in a com-mitment to the whole church body. Once the team is on that same theological page, the real fun begins.

Create a Shared Lexicon

Words matter. As George Orwell said: "If thought corrupts lan-guage, language can also corrupt thought."[8] Orwell was lament-ing poor writing, but his insight reaches far beyond that. When we use words, we connect an idea we have with an idea in someone else's head. Words are the hooks on which shared ideas, or mental models,[9] hang. Our common use of words is what shapes our shared understanding.

If you want to bring change to a community, introduce new words or phrases to the group's commonly shared lexicon. (You can also use current words and phrases in a new way, but that's a subtler change and in some ways more difficult to pull off.) Churches love to say things like "community" on a regular basis—in sermons, during prayer, in a weekly email. Your job is to explore and explain what community really means. This should be your first step in training those who are involved with your ministry, but talk to others about the idea too. Ask them to reflect on and write down words or phrases that come to mind to convey community within *every* ministry— singles, seniors, children, and so on.

What you will be doing is creating a commonly held lexicon of words and phrases that draw together everyone's idea about what this means for you. The next step is to make a fairly short list of key words and a phrase or two that everyone agrees will be the way you all describe what adoptive ministry is.

The church where I am currently serving largely shares my commitment to creating a stronger sense of community across a large and generationally separated congregation. For several years many of the leaders have been deeply engaged in my work and the Fuller Youth Institute, especially *Hurt 2.0*, *Sticky Faith*, and now *Growing Young*. The next step we have taken as a staff is to come up with words and phrases that match our aim. Here are some of them:

- adoptive
- family
- siblings
- we're in this together
- we need each other

Now every time we do anything that uses words, we try to throw in at least one of these. A week ago, during a prayer at our midweek dinner, our middle school director mentioned our "adoptive family." In the announcements last Sunday, an associate pastor said, "This week we're going to swap name tags so we can pray for our fellow siblings we just met." As the weeks and months go by, the congregation is not only getting used to hearing these (and other) words and phrases, but they are starting to use them with each other. We have only begun this process, but we can see a shared lexicon emerging just from this one simple strategy.

Share Narratives

Stories are powerful tools for adjusting our mental models of what it means to be God's people together. Set the example by talking about adoptive community in action. Show how New Testament descriptions of early congregations provide a blueprint for community. Then connect the dots to biblical forms of ministry you see taking place in your own congregation.

Occasionally when someone reads the powerful descriptions of the church in the first four chapters of the book of Acts, you may hear members saying, "People don't want that kind of community!" But God created us to find our home in his household. Whether people know it or not is a different issue. Our job is not to convince people to begin to move toward something that is foreign to their souls, or even their longings. Often they just don't know how much they crave familial connection.

And don't forget: you don't work alone. The Holy Spirit is in the business of prompting followers of Jesus toward intimate community. It's what God does. Our job is to simply do our best to respond to that prompting.

Stories are a powerful way to show even the most fearful that the kind of community the Bible talks about *is already happening here.*

Martha can't help herself, she just cares for young people. When there is a birthday, she's the one to bring the cake. When a teenager seems down, Martha's note arrives the next day (not email or text, mind you—the real deal, and nothing says to a young person I really do care than a handwritten note in the mail!). Her reputation is widespread. In a church of over a thousand people Martha is re-nowned for knowing almost every middle schooler, teenager, and emerging adult—not only their names, but their stories. When asked about why she does what she does, she scoffs and replies, "You would do the same thing, especially if you got to know them like I do." And that's the key. Martha has a heart not to "do ministry" but to know and care for young people. Welcome to the adoptive church.

I recently mentioned Martha from the pulpit so a few thousand people could hear it (I reluctantly got her permission). When I mentioned her, and she received applause, Martha was mostly embar-rassed, but later told me she was also a bit saddened. "I'm not spe-cial, they belong to me, and I to them, so I just love them. Doesn't everybody?" Martha's story, once told, helped others to begin to see themselves, their church, and their young people differently. The church is a long way from the exemplar adoptive church, but at least we're on the journey to loving the vulnerable, the lost, the young, and the outsider.

Experiment on the Edges

Narratives like Martha's can help show how an adoptive ministry approach works for one person, but building an adoptive church takes strategy and intentionality. Relational strategies are essential, but strategic and intentionally designed programming must be instituted to bring about lasting change.

The best way to move forward while avoiding the skepticism or criticism from the masses is to experiment on the margins, where there is little ownership (and interference) from those not directly involved or impacted. You can work the margins in two major ways: the invisible and the temporary.

Invisible, off-the-radar programs and events offer some of the most radical, unexpected, and innovative opportunities, all with-out disrupting normal schedules or budgets. For example, you could encourage an existing small group of high school guys to take on a few shut-in seniors from the church as their own grandparents for a semester as a replacement for their group meetings. This would likely not be on anyone's radar (except for parents, who should be included in the planning). Such experiments allow you to learn from both the young men's and the seniors' experiences. If successful, the experiment can be tweaked, expanded, and gradually embraced by the entire church.

Temporary events or programs have benefits that the off-the-grid programs do not, but they also carry greater risks. The benefits include the opportunity to bring awareness to the intentionality of exploring deeper familial relationships in a community and to broaden the buy-in for the event itself as well as demonstrating the value of trying new things in general. Any public and open experiment should be gently introduced in a way that reassures members that the church they love will not be too radically altered. The key is to make sure to connect the experiment to the intention to strengthen familial ties with one another.

For example, the introduction of "family meals" once a month, with a commitment to doing it well so that all intended participants enjoy it, is a good example of where this strategy works well. In contrast, I have seen church staff use the rationale of intergenerational community to add drums to a "traditional" service, when this kind of experiment has little if anything to do with relationally connecting people.

The risks of a creative or unique event or program should be carefully considered before moving too fast or too far. When an experiment fails or is not well received, the ability to tweak it for a second event is diminished, if not scuttled. Sometimes, public experimental initiatives actually backfire and make things worse for the community. One church, after hearing a speaker share the story of his church, decided to push their congregation into greater intimacy by lengthening services and adding a coffee break between singing and the sermon. They promoted the idea as something they were going to try for a month. After two weeks, so many people in the congregation were upset with the plan that they called a special meeting and threatened to fire the staff person leading the charge.

I suggest you do both: experiment with all-church one-time events and programs that keep the issue of communal, familial integration at the forefront of the congregation's image of what church is, while also exploring nonthreatening but outside-the-box programmatic options that can eventually be integrated into the church's regular practice.

As you do all three with care and communication where necessary, continually reinforcing the corporate lexicon and sharing the stories of how people are enjoying walking through life and faith together, you will see the adoptive family begin to emerge. Take baby steps, don't push too hard, and communicate well what you're doing and why.

Resources to Convince the Unconvinced

As we move forward with a commitment to live more fully into our adoptive family in Christ, many resources are available to us to help people embrace this move.

Spiritual Discipline of Discernment

While this may seem like a strange use of the term *resource*, theologically that is what a spiritual discipline is. God has provided for us in our freedom (Gal. 5:1) what are often called "practices" that assist us in placing ourselves into a position to receive the grace, power, and transformation that God has for us. Spiritual disciplines are best understood, then, not as "have tos" but as "get tos." Spiritual disciplines are "gifts that channel" faith and "rhythms of the Spirit."[10] Since any effort we make to enter into and embody our mutual adoption in Christ as community is the work of the Spirit, our "discipline" is to see our efforts as a way to channel that faith through prayer, Spirit-led conversation, and Spirit-empowered discernment. This is God's mission we are aligning with, and therefore as we stay fixed on a careful reading of Scripture and a sincere commitment to listening to the Spirit together, we can move forward with confidence that this is where God is leading our community.

Outside People Who Can Tell Us What We Cannot Say or Hear Ourselves

The idea of adoptive youth ministry did not emerge in a vacuum. Many others are exploring the same basic concept of seeing youth ministry through the lens of the church instead of as a stand-alone commitment of adult believers. The term *adoptive ministry*, while being used in limited circles, is not yet well known, but the driving idea behind "intergenerational ministry" has taken center stage with many youth ministry and other ecclesial leaders. One of the most important reasons, and strategies, for bringing in outside preachers and seminars is to invite them to speak into issues that a staff person or even senior pastor may not easily be able to. As someone who has done that for years on behalf of youth and family ministry, it is rather interesting to me that people can be deeply moved by an outsider about something their own preacher said only a month before with little response.

The only reason to bring in someone from the outside is to re-inforce a way of thinking or living that you have already been led to pursue. So obviously, who you bring in is just as important as what they say. The place you insert them—whether it is preaching in a service, offering a seminar to parents and others, or consulting with the lay leadership—also should be strategic and purposeful.

Other Materials That Can Foster Conversation

Lastly, do not discount any other source of input that can be used as a catalyst for further conversation. A ten-minute podcast that a small group of leaders listen to can spark a month-long discussion bringing about creative systemic change. Providing a chapter of a book (but be sure you buy the copies of everything you hand out even in copy form—the law and Christian ethics are very clear on that one!) for a Sunday school class, a group of staff, or a parents' group can lead to new ways of thinking and greater willingness to ask hard questions.

Strategies to Convince the Unconvinced

Strategy, by definition, is a hierarchical term that implies one person or party seeking to change another person or party. In seeking to be "strategic" in helping others recognize and then respond to the call of the gospel to a community, it is important to understand how much people resist someone treating them like a problem to be fixed or a puzzle to be solved. Our goal in leading a church or organization to change how it thinks about and serves young people is to engage in the process of moving people to the point of being willing to look at something they might otherwise ignore in order to eventually embrace what this might mean for everyone involved. Yet people do not want to be subject to a strategy, and when they feel that they are, they resist and flee.

While we may believe that we are not responsible for someone else's defensiveness, how we approach people whom we are asking to consider change can make a difference in how they receive not only our message but also us as people. Research into the ways that people receive new and potentially difficult ideas has revealed behaviors and attitudes that generally promote a defensive reaction from a recipient of a message. Researcher Jack Gibb details these in what he labels six behaviors (or attitudes) that create a "Defensive Climate":[11]

- superiority
- certainty
- evaluation of opponents
- control
- neutrality
- strategy

While most people will blame defensiveness on the "other," more than likely if any one of these behaviors or attitudes is picked up by a person, then, all things being equal, their reaction will be defensive. So, although "strategy" is one of the six behaviors that can elicit a defensive response, our best course is to seek to avoid these by doing the opposite of each behavior.

1. *Being a peer versus superiority.* If someone senses that we think we are smarter than they are and that's why we need to tell them what to think or how to live, our inclination will be to immediately resist what they have to say. Every person wants to connect with someone whom they believe is a peer, or better yet, a friend. Our attitude toward the other is telepathic, and so whenever we try to convince or especially change someone's thinking our best place to start is by coming alongside them as a friend.

2. *Conviction versus certainty.* People don't resist conviction, but they hate certainty. When our commitment to our ideas slips into our speech in such a way that it communicates that there are no alternative ways to think or believe, walls go up and people shut down. I may be thoroughly convinced that I am right about something, but when I am in dialogue or even presenting to a group in a one-way forum, I must allow for space for others to consider what *they* think even as I am sharing what *I* think. This is difficult for some of us because we might actually believe that there are no other ways to think. But unless we are careful that attitude buried deep within us will eke out in ways that will hinder our ability to get someone to even consider what we are saying. Conviction is a powerful form of persuading someone (a biblical form of sharing the gospel to others, as Paul says in 2 Corinthians 5:11), yet we have to remember that others are usually equally convicted about their perspective, and therefore to help bring change our first step is to find ways to allow for multiple perspectives to get on the table before us and go from there.

3. *Sharing my story versus evaluation of opponents.* We are built to hear and tell stories. Stories have a way of connecting us to one another. When we seek to persuade, a common trap we can fall into is communicating through words or even body language that we "know what you think" about a given issue or topic. When we share our own perspective through story, we stay focused on our genuine commitment without telling anyone else that we "get" them. In doing this, others may be more easily drawn in to what we are saying.

4. *Conversation versus control.* In a conversation control has many forms. When we are trying to convince someone of something that they do not yet buy in to we can easily—if we're not careful—appear to be trying to control the time to win over the other person. Control can be experienced as anything from a rapid-fire nonstop monologue to constant interrupting or even speaking and then impatiently waiting until the other person is done talking. One ironic thing about how most of us talk to one another is that we are often so committed to being heard that we engage in such a way that we cease to actually listen. In contrast, the point of a conversation is to enter into a shared experience of knowing and being known. When we so badly want to "change" someone else without caring where they are coming from or what their experience is, we become nothing but a one-way message, take it or leave it. No wonder people get defensive.

5. *Care about the person versus neutrality.* What is our goal at all times as we engage with each other? To care not only about our perspective but also to honestly and deliberately care about the other's. That we call conversation. We might think, then, that our best course of action in persuasion is to remain neutral with an issue. The reality is if we *try* to express neutrality when we really are not, then we chance being perceived as manipulative or deceptive. If we really *are* neutral, then in fact what we are

doing is not persuading but exploring. That's not a bad thing, but it is a different motive for the conversation. In addition, nobody wants to talk to someone who doesn't seem to care one way or another. We don't have to be neutral, we have to simply care as we communicate.

6. *Authentic connection versus being strategic.* If we come across as anything but authentic when we are trying to convince someone to consider a different point of view or a new way of thinking, we risk missing the chance to truly engage the heart and mind of the other person. In other words, these six behaviors indicate that if we are trying to be "strategic" to convince someone that they are wrong and that they need to change, even by appearing to be "strategic" we have lost our opportunity for dialogue. And in so doing we often push people even further away from our intended perspective than before we started.

The Scriptures address this same issue this way: "Always be prepared to give an answer to everyone who asks you to give the reason for the hope that you have. But do this with gentleness and respect" (1 Pet. 3:15). It is not our job to convince someone how to think, even in leadership in the church. It is our job to be faithful to the gospel as both Scripture and the Holy Spirit reveal, and to present our thoughts in a way that is neither manipulative nor arrogant. We are called to be gentle and respectful, even with those whom we believe are dead wrong.

These "strategies," then, are how we present our perspective when given the platform or opportunity to help people see who we all are in Christ and what it means to live as the church as mutually adopted siblings.

The Power of Casual Conversations

Consider a person who you believe may stand in the way of substantive change in how your church looks at and treats teenagers and young adults. Even before speaking with them, you might feel that they would not be open to thinking or behaving differently than how the church has in the past. With anyone who you believe is an important player in making a systemic shift in how we think about and serve the young, the first objective is to seek them out in safe, reflective conversation.

I have come to picture persuasion as sitting with someone with whom I may have a disagreement, and it is my job to convince her of something. Typically, when we get the opportunity to discuss something important with a person we believe is (or even could be) an adversary, we think of a dialogue as a debate where both parties take turns making their case to an unknown crowd from separate podiums. Even if we were to use the imagery of a conversation, we might only change the venue and audience slightly by picturing ourselves and the other on different sides of a picnic table. Still, we might approach the conversation as a back-and-forth, tit-for-tat, two-person debate on the given merits of our positions.

At the end of the day, the worst form of communication and persuasion is the one-way, "I'm right, you're wrong" approach. So even with your most vocal opponent, your best way to create a productive dialogue—and hopefully bring the opportunity for growth and change for both of you—is to get up from your side of the picnic table and take a seat alongside your friend. Then look at each other as you listen and share, with conviction, what you think matters—especially when Jesus is brought into the middle of the relationship as well as the conversation.

Appendix

ADOPTIVE CHURCH 101

You probably have never heard the phrase "adoptive ministry." It is not a common way to talk about ministry. The word *adoption* is usually used to refer to an adult or a couple who searches for and adopts a child into their family. At first glance "adoptive ministry," and especially "adoptive *youth* ministry," would imply that our job in the church is to "adopt" kids. Frankly, that's how I first thought of it. But after sharing the idea with others and spending time thinking about it, I came to see that adoption in the Bible primarily refers to God adopting us as we trust in Jesus (John 1:12). So what you will see throughout this book is a perspective on ministry that begins with God's gift of adoption to everyone who calls on him by faith. Adoptive ministry, then, is how we learn to live into this reality.

As you read this book, there might be words, phrases, or ideas that you may not remember from a previous section, or that may simply not make sense to you. (That happens to me a lot when I read a book, and I do this for a living!) So keep these pages handy if you get a little lost in key concepts or terms, or run across a word or phrase that throws you. Think of it like the glossary in a technical book from school—as a helpful way to keep things straight.

Three Key Concepts/Characteristics of an Adoptive Church

- Adoptive ministry is a way of thinking about ministry as encouraging a community of people who have been adopted into God's household to intentionally live that out together as his children.

- Adoptive ministry encourages those who feel like they are already included in the local family (usually called "the church") to be the ones to build bridges of welcome and participation to those who might not feel connected or valued.

- Adoptive ministry takes seriously two essential commitments: to *nurture* those who need guidance and care, and to *empower* those who generally do not participate in and contribute to the life of the whole body.

Biblical Foundations of an Adoptive Church

- "Yet to all who did receive him, to those who believed in his name, he gave the right to become children of God" (John 1:12; *notice the move from the singular "to all" to the plural "children"*).

- "For he chose us in him before the creation of the world to be holy and blameless in his sight. In love he predestined us for adoption to sonship through Jesus Christ, in accordance with his pleasure and will" (Eph. 1:4–5; *"adoption to sonship" is a technical term including males and females*).

- "But when the set time had fully come, God sent his Son, born of a woman, born under the law, to redeem those under the law, that we might receive adoption to sonship. Because you are his children, God sent the Spirit of his Son into our hearts, the Spirit who calls out, 'Abba, Father'" (Gal. 4:4–6; *notice the plural "you"*).

- Three other texts where Paul uses this same phrase "adopted to sonship" (Greek, *huiothesia*): Romans 8:15, 23; 9:4.

- Texts where our life together is described as a family:

  Matthew 12:46–50

  Galatians 6:10

  Ephesians 2:19

  1 Thessalonians 4:10

  1 Timothy 3:15

  Hebrews 2:10–12

  1 Peter 2:27; 5:9

- The Old Testament is about "God's people," and as such living as "children of God" is the theme throughout. There are particular texts, however, that directly point to this idea (this is just a sampling):

  Exodus 4:22

  Deuteronomy 14:1; 27:9; 28:10

  2 Samuel 7:14

  1 Chronicles 22:7–10; 28:6

  Psalm 82:6

  Isaiah 43:6; 63:8, 16

  Jeremiah 3:19; 31:9

  Hosea 1:9–10; 11:1

- New Testament texts referring to the teachings on "one another" (this is just a sampling):

  Romans 12:10, 16; 13:8; 14:3; 15:7, 14

  1 Corinthians 1:10

  2 Corinthians 3:11

  Galatians 5:13

  Ephesians 4:2, 32; 5:19, 21

  Philippians 2:1–11

  Colossians 3:13–16

  1 Thessalonians 4:9, 18; 5:11

Hebrews 3:13; 10:24–25; 13:1

1 Peter (the whole book)

1 John (the whole book)

Why Adoptive Ministry Is an Important Grounding for Youth Ministry

I believe that youth ministry needs a biblical grounding and trajectory to base our work and practices on. As young people come to faith in Christ, their greatest chance at making the relationship last is ultimately to discover that the church is their home on earth. The Bible is clear that we are alone, or even orphaned, until we turn our lives around and come to sincere faith in Jesus Christ. When we come to faith, we are given the "right to become" God's children (John 1:12). That means we move from being alone to being in a new family. This family is what God has intended from the beginning. He is our heavenly parent, we now call him "Father" (*Abba*), and we are also siblings with everybody else who trusts in Christ. Lots of people, especially young people, who come to faith in Christ remain alone. They may give their life to Christ and grow to trust him, but they may never know that the Christian journey is meant to be lived in community. Thus, adoptive ministry is a way to ensure we keep at the forefront the fact that we all belong together and need each other to help us live into that truth.

Going Deeper

In Christian circles we use words like *body*, *community*, and *fellowship*. In bringing *adopted siblings* into the mix of that language, we become more aware of the depth of relationship that God has for us and has called us to. To go deeper in examining ideas related to adoptive ministry, I suggest you read the work of Christian forebears who wrote extensively on Christian community. On the pages of their works, you'll see glimpses of "adoptive ministry" described long before the term was ever circulated. My favorites are Dietrich Bonhoeffer, Karl Barth, Jean Vanier, Henri J. M. Nouwen, and Dallas Willard.

Questions That Have Come Up regarding Adoptive Ministry

As I finalized this work on adoptive youth ministry, I sent the draft manuscript to a select group of people I know and trust to get their take. Did it make sense? Was my logic clear? And most important, is this book a helpful resource to move the church to reflect on how it thinks about and treats the young?

Of all the comments (and there were many), one person in particular took the time to dig in to the heart of the matter. In our back-and-forth, I came to see how his impressions of the book were perhaps what others, maybe many others, might see as they read. So, after adding a few thoughts and with this friend's agreement, I include this conversation here to make as clear as possible my ideas for adoptive ministry. While this is not our verbatim conversation, this represents what my friend was interested in talking about.

Adoption as a Grounding Concept

Friend: Thanks for sending the manuscript. I do believe that it has potential for making a significant impact on youth ministry and on the church. But I do have some questions, more perhaps "wonderings," that I'd like to discuss with you.

My biggest wondering is about your adoption metaphor. I wonder if you have been as clear as you want to be. I ask this for three reasons: (1) it will help the reader know exactly what you mean; (2) it will help the reader understand how this is a call for a philosophical shift (otherwise they'll keep saying, "Oh, I do that already"); and (3) it'll also clarify your applications in the later chapters.

Chap: Thanks for this. First, it is not my metaphor, it's Paul's. The idea of who we are as adopted siblings just hasn't been applied in the church regarding those on the outside of the dominant center of a church community (which is one major reason I believe he used the metaphor, to bring unity to a fracturing church).

Also, adoptive ministry is less of a shift and more of a trajectory, or target. When we pursue what we call "intergenerational" ministry, often we are talking more about a program or strategy than a theological outcome or even reason for it. In contrast, that is what adoptive youth ministry is. To me youth ministry has seemed to not be as concerned with the outcome of our ministry as inclusion in, and being embedded within, the body of Christ. Even if we are working to make sure adults take kids more seriously and include them in ministry opportunities, if we don't have a driving theological *rationale* that leads us to seek that for every young person, we will invite the young to Christ without offering them inclusion in the family that God has for them. That's what adoptive youth ministry is about.

Adoption as a Metaphor

Friend: What is the opposite of "adopted"? You suggest that it is "orphaned." Is that true? If so, who has been "orphaned"? And how have we/they been orphaned?

Chap: Theologically, we have all been orphaned by and through the fall and in our own participation in it. It is, as James Dunn puts it, "the decisive and universal character of man's fall."[1] Thus, as a consequence, sin results in what Dietrich Bonhoeffer called "a concept of separation."[2]

Friend: Can we adopt each other if we're siblings? Don't parents adopt?

Chap: "Adoptive ministry" does not *replace* the family, but it *describes* the family and household of God. So yes, parents adopt. In the church we don't theologically *adopt* each other. Rather, we encourage one another as adopted siblings (John 1:12).

Friend: Does adoption have any definition beyond a relational one? Is there a legal one? What is the difference between God adopting, a parent adopting, or a community adopting?

Chap: God adopting us is the gift of the incarnation. Parents adopting a child is bringing them into a social family unit, which is a different application of the notion of adoption. Again, communities of faith don't adopt; they encourage those who are adopted by God. In addition, adoptive ministry has implications for evangelism, for we also see all human beings as those whom God loves but are yet to be given the right to be God's adopted children.

Friend: What are the limitations to this metaphor that you want to name so that people don't discredit it (as all metaphors have limits)?

Chap: I honestly do not see any limitations at all, so long as we use the term *adopted* the way the Scriptures do. The fact is that moving from orphan to adopted child among other children is who we are in Christ (Matt. 12:48–50; John 1:12—two significant texts for this).

Jesus

Friend: Did Jesus use adoptive language? If so, how did he demonstrate it? I think of the moment at the cross where he gives John to his mother and his mother to John. Is that adoptive?

Chap: I like that reference to John. And yes, in Matthew 12:48–50 when Mary and Jesus's brothers came to speak to him, he said, "Who is my mother?" Also, in the passage on the sheep and goats in Matthew 25:40, where Jesus identifies with the vulnerable and those in need, he calls them his "brothers and sisters." (Throughout most of church history it was taught that these had to be Christians because nonbelievers could not be his brothers and sisters. Dale Bruner in his Matthew commentary points out that the majority of current scholars affirm the universality of the sibling label;[3] I agree, but mostly because the text is eschatological, so I refer to them as "imminent siblings," like an acorn is an imminent oak tree.)

Intergenerational versus Adoptive

Friend: Is intergenerational . . . adoptive? And if not, what's the difference?

Chap: *Intergenerational* is a word we use programmatically, and maybe strategically (or perhaps missionally, although I don't recall seeing it used that way). *Adoptive* encompasses intergenerational connectedness, but it goes way deeper and also reduces, if not removes, the generational hierarchy that can remain. A powerful force against adoptive ministry is generational, or positional, hierarchy. As siblings we are called to demonstrate respect and nurturing love toward one another, but our general rule of life together can be summed up in Philippians 2:3–4: "Do nothing out of selfish ambition or vain conceit. Rather, in humility value others above yourselves, not looking to your own interests but each of you to the interests of the others."

NOTES

Welcome to the Adoptive Church

1. Scott Wilcher, *The Orphaned Generation: The Father's Heart for Connecting Youth and Young Adults to Your Church* (Chesapeake, VA: The Upstream Project, 2010), 147.

2. An example of this is found in Chap Clark, "The Changing Face of Adolescence: A Theological View of Human Development" and "The Myth of the Perfect Youth Ministry Model," in *Starting Right: Thinking Theologically about Youth Ministry*, ed. Kenda Creasy Dean, Chap Clark, and Dave Rahn (Grand Rapids: Zondervan, 2001), 41–62 and 109–24, respectively.

Chapter 1 Creating an Adoptive Youth Ministry

1. See Rom. 8:15–16, 23–24; 9:3–4; Gal. 4:4–7; Eph. 1:4–6.

2. Rom. 8:15 and Gal. 4:6. D. F. Payne, "Abba," in *New Bible Dictionary*, 3rd ed., ed. D. R. W. Wood, I. H. Marshall, A. R. Millard, J. I. Packer, and D. J. Wiseman (Downers Grove, IL: InterVarsity, 1996), 2. Also consider this statement by James Dunn: "And although his claims have to be qualified, and oversentimentalizing deductions have too often been drawn from them, it is still justified to assert that Jesus' use of 'Abba' most probably implies a sense of intimate sonship on the part of Jesus, expressed as it was in the colloquial language of close family relationship." James D. G. Dunn, *Romans 1–8*, Word Biblical Commentary 38A (Dallas: Word, 1988), 453–54.

3. A phrase used for believers in Rom. 8:1 and throughout the New Testament epistles.

Chapter 2 Adoptive Youth Ministry

1. Kenda Creasy Dean, Chap Clark, and Dave Rahn, eds., *Starting Right: Thinking Theologically about Youth Ministry* (Grand Rapids: Zondervan, 2001).

2. Mark Senter, ed., *Four Views of Youth Ministry and the Church* (Grand Rapids: Zondervan / Youth Specialties Academic, 2001). In addition to Mark Senter, authors included Chap Clark, Wesley Black, and South African Malan Nel.

3. In the chapter "The Myth of the Perfect Model of Youth Ministry" in Dean, Clark, and Rahn, *Starting Right*, I called "assimilation . . . the ultimate goal of any youth ministry program" (121). In the chapter "The Missional Approach to Youth Ministry" in Senter, *Four Views*, I defined youth ministry as "a *mission* of the church with an end goal of full assimilation into the locally expressed body of Christ" (87).

4. There is abundant research affirming this trend. Two of the more prominent examples are Kara E. Powell and Chap Clark, *Sticky Faith: Everyday Ideas to Build Lasting Faith in Your Kids* (Grand Rapids: Zondervan, 2011); and David Kinnaman and Aly Hawkins, *You Lost Me: Why Young Christians Are Leaving Church and Rethinking Faith* (Grand Rapids: Baker Books, 2016).

5. For more information on Fuller Youth Institute's Sticky Faith initiatives and products, see https://fulleryouthinstitute.org/stickyfaith.

6. Powell and Clark, *Sticky Faith*. The second book from FYI, similar to the first but targeted to a different audience, is *Sticky Faith, Youth Worker Edition: Practical Ideas to Nurture Long-Term Faith in Teenagers*, by Kara E. Powell, Brad M. Griffin, and Cheryl A. Crawford (Grand Rapids: Zondervan, 2011).

7. Powell and Clark, *Sticky Faith*, 15.

8. Chap Clark, *Hurt 2.0: Inside the World of Today's Teenagers*, 2nd ed. (Grand Rapids: Baker Academic, 2011).

9. The report can be found at http://hemorrhagingfaith.com.

10. See Clark, *Hurt 2.0*; Robert D. Putnam, *Our Kids: The American Dream in Crisis* (New York: Simon & Schuster, 2016); and David Elkind, *The Hurried Child: Growing Up Too Fast Too Soon* (Boston: Da Capo Press, 2006), for comprehensive evidence for the stress and struggle that nearly every child, adolescent, and emerging adult experiences growing up in contemporary Western society.

11. Elkind, *Hurried Child*, 3.

Chapter 3 Creating Environments Where Faith Families Flourish

1. See, for example, Michael Lipka, "A Closer Look at America's Rapidly Growing Religious 'Nones'," *FactTank*, Pew Research Center, May 13, 2015, http://www.pewresearch.org/fact-tank/2015/05/13/a-closer-look-at-americas-rapidly-growing-religious-nones/.

2. Ed Stetzer, "Growing Young," *Christianity Today*, October 28, 2016, http://www.christianitytoday.com/edstetzer/2016/october/growing-young.html. The article is an interview with Kara Powell based on the groundbreaking study described in Kara Powell, Jake Mulder, and Brad Griffin, *Growing Young: Six Essential Strategies to Help Young People Discover and Love Your Church* (Grand Rapids: Baker Books, 2016).

3. *Merriam-Webster*, s.v. "nurture," https://www.merriam-webster.com/dictionary/nurture.

4. *Oxford English Dictionary*, s.v. "nurture," https://en.oxforddictionaries.com/definition/nurture. ·

5. Henri J. M. Nouwen, Donald P. McNeill, and Douglas A. Morrison, *Compassion: A Reflection on the Christian Life* (New York: Image Books, 1983), 4.

6. Powell, Mulder, and Griffin, *Growing Young*, 53.

Chapter 4 Making Disciples among Siblings

1. Dallas Willard, *The Spirit of the Disciplines: Understanding How God Changes Lives* (San Francisco: HarperSanFrancisco, 1991), 20.

2. The Greek word used in John 6:29, *pisteuō*, is almost always translated "believe," and sometimes "have faith" and "trust."

3. In Mark's Gospel the "seed" is used overtly for both people and the word (4:14–15). Matthew softens this a bit but implies the same (13:19–23). "Despite the slight mixing of images, the point remains clear. (Matthew has thus not avoided the mixed images in Mark 4:14 and 16 [where the seed is equated with the person].)" Donald A. Hagner, *Matthew 1–13*, Word Biblical Commentary 33A (Dallas: Word, 1998), 380.

4. There are several instances of the call to repent, or turn from one direction to another. See, for example, Acts 3:19.

5. This is basic Christian theology, and one clear example of this is found in Gal. 5, especially vv. 5–6, where we focus on our faith, or trust, and we wait for God's Spirit to change us into people who are characterized by love, or righteousness.

6. I acknowledge that Eph. 4 (as well as other texts) says the ultimate end of discipleship is that we would "become mature," yet even in this passage the image is that of organic growth toward maturity as opposed to the end of actualizing full or complete maturity. While some traditions believe that it is theoretically possible to achieve Christlike maturity, in practice and in my experience we are all on the road, some moving more deliberately than others, toward maturity in Christ.

7. A. W. Tozer, *The Set of the Sail* (Chicago: Moody, 2007), 12.

8. John Calvin, *Institutes of the Christian Religion*, ed. John T. McNeill, trans. Ford Lewis Battles (Philadelphia: Westminster, 1960), 1:70 (§1.6.1).

9. G. F. Hawthorne, *Philippians*, Word Biblical Commentary 43 (Dallas: Word, 2004), 197.

10. See also Mark 12:29–30 and Luke 10:27.

11. The earliest believers were called "followers of the Way" and only later began to be called Christians. See Acts 9:2 and 11:26. "From Acts 9:2; 19:9, 23; 22:4; 24:14, 22 we learn that 'the Way' was the oldest designation of the Christian church for itself. This is partly an extension of a use already found in the OT; *cf.* Is. 40:3 with 40:10–11, where God's people are seen being led along God's way." H. L. Ellison, "Way," in *New Bible Dictionary*, 3rd ed., ed. D. R. W. Wood, I. H. Marshall, A. R. Millard, J. I. Packer, and D. J. Wiseman (Downers Grove, IL: InterVarsity, 1996), 1233.

12. Dallas Willard, *The Divine Conspiracy: Rediscovering Our Hidden Life in God* (San Francisco: Harper, 1998).

13. As noted above, the word *trust* is *pisteuō*, which is usually translated "have faith" or "believe." *Pisteuō* is translated "faith" in Rom. 14:2 ("One person's *faith* allows them to eat anything"), "believe" in Rom. 6:8 ("Now if we died with Christ, we *believe* that we will also live with him"), and "trust" in 1 Cor. 13:7 ("[Love] always protects, always *trusts*, always hopes"). Other Greek words are closely associated with

pisteuō, among them *pistis* and *peithō*. In the New Testament (NIV) this root word and its derivatives are translated "faith" or "believe/belief" hundreds of times and "trust" only twenty times, most often for the concept of someone or something being deemed "trustworthy." For some reason biblical scholars and translators seem to be more comfortable with the terms *faith* and *belief* than with *trust*. This conversation, however, is beyond the scope of this book.

Chapter 5 The Goal of Ministry in an Adoptive Church

1. This is confirmed in repeated studies on social environments. In the research project "Churches That Engage Young People" from Fuller Theological Seminary's Fuller Youth Institute, warmth was a prominent feature of churches that young people reported appreciating. For more on this, see Kara Powell, Jake Mulder, and Brad Griffin, *Growing Young: Six Essential Strategies to Help Young People Discover and Love Your Church* (Grand Rapids: Baker Books, 2016).

2. Wayne Rice, *Up Close and Personal: How to Build Community in Your Youth Group* (El Cajon, CA: Youth Specialties, 1989).

3. *Merriam-Webster*, s.v. "atomize," https://www.merriam-webster.com/diction ary/atomize.

4. The evidence for this has been overwhelmingly documented by a variety of scholars, the most prominent being Harvard's Robert D. Putnam. Two publications that detail the data are *Bowling Alone: The Collapse and Revival of American Community* (New York: Touchstone, 2001) and *Our Kids: The American Dream in Crisis* (New York: Simon & Schuster, 2016). For youth ministry application, see the summary of Chap Clark's ethnographic research in *Hurt 2.0: Inside the World of Today's Teenagers*, 2nd ed. (Grand Rapids: Baker Academic, 2011).

Part Two The Structure of an Adoptive Church

1. A reference to a common expression in Jim Collins's *Good to Great: Why Some Companies Make the Leap and Others Don't* (New York: HarperBusiness, 2001).

Chapter 6 Implementing Adoptive Youth Ministry

1. Carl E. Larson and Frank M. J. LaFasto, *Teamwork: What Must Go Right, What Can Go Wrong* (Newbury Park, CA: Sage, 1989).

2. Actor and writer Peter Ustinov is credited with this statement, but I have not been able to track down the source. I first wrote this in a paper for my doctoral studies and have relied on it as a broad-stroke descriptor ever since. The essence of it is that communication is more than speaking or delivery of content; it is taking responsibility for how a message is heard and received.

3. Currently there is a sweeping movement in response to the Fuller Youth Institute's (FYI) Growing Young corpus and training, which is enabling hundreds of churches to apply what FYI calls "six essential strategies to help young people discover and love your church" (the subtitle of the book *Growing Young*, by Kara Powell, Jake Mulder, and Brad Griffin [Grand Rapids: Baker Books, 2016]). These strategies are not especially new, but they have been shown by FYI's research to be the characteristics of those churches that young people (defined as fifteen- to twenty-nine-year-olds) report as being what

draws them and keeps them invested in a given faith community. This is an important body of research, and I applaud my colleagues at FYI for their continuing work to help churches become sensitive and more committed to including and welcoming the young.

4. This is an old, telling expression that actually comes from Eccles. 10:1, "As dead flies give perfume a bad smell . . ." J. B. Phillips's New Testament translation uses this quote in Rom. 9.

5. I use the phrase "in Christ" with quotation marks around it because of the profound theological import of the phrase. In this book I do not have time to unpack the current perspectives and nuances that this little phrase elicits, but there is widespread agreement among theologians that it is important in believers' understanding of how everything changes when we believe in Jesus Christ.

6. Ronald A. Heifetz, Alexander Grashow, and Marty Linsky, *The Practice of Adaptive Leadership: Tools and Tactics for Changing Your Organization and the World* (Cambridge, MA: Harvard Business Press, 2009).

Chapter 7 The Power of Partners

1. Sarah Alexander, "First among Equals: A New Approach to Leadership," *Management-Issues.com*, December 12, 2013, http://www.management-issues.com /opinion/6824/first-among-equals-a-new-approach-to-leadership/. For another example of this use in business, see Boris Veldhuijzen van Zanten, "The Difference between a Leader and a Primus Inter Pares," *Entrepreneur*, September 7, 2011, https:// thenextweb.com/entrepreneur/2011/09/07/the-difference-between-a-leader-and-a -primus-inter-pares/.

2. Bill MacPhee, "Adoptive Leadership," in *Adoptive Youth Ministry*, ed. Chap Clark (Grand Rapids: Baker Academic, 2016), 285. In this section MacPhee also provides Doug Fields's list for moving a volunteer from initial interest to full inclusion as a youth ministry volunteer (*Purpose Driven Youth Ministry* [Grand Rapids: Zondervan, 1998], 292–98).

3. MacPhee, "Adoptive Leadership," 286.

Chapter 8 Building Your Ministry Team

1. Carl E. Larson and Frank M. J. LaFasto, *Teamwork: What Must Go Right, What Can Go Wrong* (Newbury Park, CA: Sage, 1989).

2. Larson and LaFasto, *Teamwork*, 136.

3. Larson and LaFasto, *Teamwork*, 25.

4. Larson and LaFasto, *Teamwork*, 29. This "Collaborative Team Member rating sheet" is a helpful tool for any team, especially if there seem to be obstacles keeping people from working collaboratively.

5. Samuel Moore, Cameron Neylon, Martin Paul Eve, Daniel Paul O'Donnell, and Damian Pattinson, "'Excellence R Us': University Research and the Fetishisation of Excellence," *Palgrave Communications* 3 (2017): 2–3, https://ssrn.com/abstract=2902596.

Chapter 9 Nurture and the Ministry of Going

1. Although the NIV translates 1 Thess. 2:7 as "we were like young children among you," there is ample evidence that just as easily this can be translated as I have,

"gentle among you." F. F. Bruce translates the passage similarly in his commentary, "but we showed ourselves gentle among you." *1 and 2 Thessalonians*, Word Biblical Commentary 45 (Dallas: Word, 1998), 31.

2. There is a small but vocal band of people who have gone after the play and humor of youth ministry staples, especially in groups like Young Life and Youth for Christ. It is my view that these people have never actually had to walk with disinterested or beaten-down students who do not come to us with much trust.

3. Kara Powell, Jake Mulder, and Brad Griffin, *Growing Young: Six Essential Strategies to Help Young People Discover and Love Your Church* (Grand Rapids: Baker Books, 2016), 165.

Chapter 10 Beyond Participation

1. "Title IX—General Provisions," US department of Education, Paragraph 22, last revised September 15, 2004, https://www2.ed.gov/policy/elsec/leg/esea02/pg107.html.

2. "A Brief History of Gifted and Talented Education," National Association for Gifted Children, http://www.nagc.org/resources-publications/resources/gifted-education -us/brief-history-gifted-and-talented-education.

3. According to the National Center for Education Statistics, "In 2014–15, the number of children and youth ages 3–21 receiving special education services was 6.6 million, or 13 percent of all public school students. Among children and youth receiving special education services, 35 percent had specific learning disabilities." "Children and Youth with Disabilities," last updated May 2017, https://nces.ed.gov /programs/coe/indicator_cgg.asp.

4. See Kara Powell, Jake Mulder, and Brad Griffin, *Growing Young: Six Essential Strategies to Help Young People Discover and Love Your Church* (Grand Rapids: Baker Books, 2016), 50–87.

5. Holly Catterton Allen and Christine Lawton, *Intergenerational Christian Formation: Bringing the Whole Church Together in Ministry, Community and Worship* (Downers Grove, IL: InterVarsity, 2012), 270.

6. Powell, Mulder, and Griffin, *Growing Young*, 50–87.

Chapter 11 Adoptive Youth Ministry and the Challenge of Change

1. Stanley Grenz and Jay T. Smith, *Created for Community: Connecting Christian Belief with Christian Living*, 3rd ed. (Grand Rapids: Baker Academic, 2014), 210.

2. Scott Cormode, *Making Spiritual Sense: Christian Leaders as Spiritual Interpreters* (Nashville: Abingdon, 2006), x–xi.

3. Scott Cormode, lecture, *Growing Young* cohort training, Fuller Theological Seminary, Pasadena, CA, October 27, 2018.

4. "Children and Youth With Disabilities," National Center for Educational Statistics, last updated April 18, 2018, https://nces.ed.gov/programs/coe/indicator_cgg.asp.

5. Robert D. Putnam, *Making Democracy Work: Civic Traditions in Modern Italy*, 2nd ed. (Princeton: Princeton University Press, 1994), 8.

6. Scott Cormode, "The Next Faithful Step," Fuller Theological Seminary, accessed August 14, 2016, http://leadership.fuller.edu/Leadership/Resources/Part_4 -Leading_for_Transformative_Change/I__Technical_and_Adaptive_Change.aspx (no longer available online).

7. Cormode, "The Next Faithful Step."

8. George Orwell, "Politics and the English Language," 1946, http://www.resort .com/~prime8/Orwell/patee.html.

9. The authors of a comprehensive article exploring the notion of mental models write, "The notion of a shared mental model is well known in the literature regarding team work among humans. It has been used to explain team functioning. The idea is that team performance improves if team members have a shared understanding of the task that is to be performed and of the involved team work." C. M. Jonker, M. B. van Riemsdijk, and B. Vermeulen, "Shared Mental Models: A Conceptual Analysis," in *Coordination, Organizations, Institutions, and Norms in Agent Systems VI*, ed. M. De Vos, N. Fornara, J. V. Pitt, and G. Vouros, Lecture Notes in Computer Science 6541 (Berlin: Springer, 2011), 132–51, quotation on 132, https://link.springer.com/book /10.1007/978-3-642-21268-0.

10. James K. A. Smith, *You Are What You Love: The Spiritual Power of Habit* (Grand Rapids: Brazos, 2016), 147, 152.

11. J. R. Gibb, "Defensive Communication," in *Communication Theory*, 2nd ed., ed. C. D. Mortensen (New Brunswick, NJ: Transaction Publishers, 201–12). See also Gibb's 1988 paper "Defensive Communication," http://reagle.org/joseph/2010/conflict /media/gibb-defensive-communication.html.

Appendix

1. James D. G. Dunn, *Romans 1–8*, Word Biblical Commentary 38A (Dallas: Word, 1998), 167.

2. Dietrich Bonhoeffer, *Theological Education Underground: 1937–1940*, vol. 15 of *Dietrich Bonhoeffer Works* (Minneapolis: Fortress, 2012), 344.

3. Frederick Dale Bruner, *Matthew: A Commentary*, vol. 2, *The Churchbook: Matthew 13–28*, rev. ed. (Grand Rapids: Eerdmans, 2004), 574–76.

INDEX

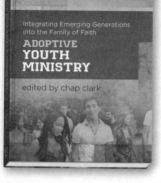
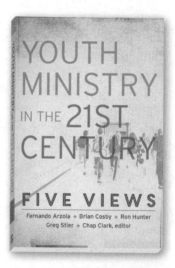